# The Good City

*Writers*

*Explore*

*21st-Century*

*Boston*

# The Good City

Edited by

Emily Hiestand

and

Ande Zellman

BEACON 150

Beacon Press

Boston

BEACON PRESS
25 Beacon Street
Boston, Massachusetts 02108-2892
www.beacon.org

Beacon Press books
are published under the auspices of
the Unitarian Universalist Association of Congregations.

08 07 06 05 04    8 7 6 5 4 3 2 1

This book is printed on acid-free paper that meets the uncoated
paper ANSI/NISO specifications for permanence as revised in 1992.

Text design by Kit Kuntze
Composition by Wilsted & Taylor Publishing Services

Cover image: Leonard P. Zakim Bunker Hill Bridge photographed by Stanley Rowin

Library of Congress Cataloging-in-Publication Data

The good city : writers explore 21st-century Boston /
edited by Emily Hiestand and Ande Zellman.
    p. cm.
ISBN 0-8070-7143-9 (pbk. : alk. paper)
1. Boston (Mass.)—Description and travel. 2. Boston (Mass.)—Social life and
customs. 3. City and town life—Massachusetts—Boston. 4. Boston (Mass.)—
Politics and government. I. Hiestand, Emily. II. Zellman, Ande.

F73.35.G66 2004
917.44'61—dc22                                    2004004642

# Contents

# Introduction:
# The Comeback City

*Paul S. Grogan*

Americans have always been ambivalent, at best, about their cities. I blame Thomas Jefferson for this, who famously declared that "cities contain all that is pestilential to the health and morals of mankind." And since the time Jefferson said that, cities have occupied a very different—and lesser—place in the American psyche than they do in the European mind.

At no time was American wariness about the urban world more apparent than in the first three decades after World War II, when every major established American city went into precipitous decline. Indeed, for most of my lifetime words like "decline" and "crisis" and "disinvestment" have been associated so often with the word "urban" as to leave a lasting impression on the imagination.

Boston participated fully and deeply in the postwar urban decline, with the usual markers: the wholesale exodus of people and then jobs to the suburbs, widespread blight and abandonment, runaway crime, racial conflict, failing schools, and so on—the whole sorry catalogue of the unsolved problems of American life.

*The Unheavenly City,* a book by the urbanist Edward Banfield published in 1970, presented both the intractability of the situation and the expectation that it would all proceed indefinitely toward some awful terminus. Some even argued that, well, we didn't need cities anymore—after all, they were the artifacts of an earlier economic paradigm; and in typical American fashion, weren't we inventing in the suburbs some new and superior form of social organization?

How lovely it is, then, to deliver in this volume a kind of eloquent rebuke to those who wrote off the American city. Whatever else these marvelous essays say, their overwhelming message is that Boston is wonderfully, dynamically alive. And it is alive above all else because this city understood how to restore and replenish what is special and distinctive about the urban experience. It turns out that not only can our culture not do without cities, but cities play an indispensable and unduplicated role in nourishing our civilization. It is no accident that we could assemble such astonishing writers here, who all bear witness to the life of the city and their often complex relationship with it.

\*  \*  \*

Only cities create and sustain the great symphonies, museums, theaters, and universities. Only cities are magnets for the creative talent and innovation that talent produces. All that and more is on sparkling display in Boston today.

It is getting harder and harder to remember the bad old days, but they really weren't that long ago. The Harvard economist Edward Glaeser has written that "an urban observer looking at Boston in 1980 would have every reason to believe that it would go the way of Detroit and Syracuse and continue along its sad path towards urban irrelevance."

Just a few years before that, in 1975, Mayor Kevin White was dreaming up the renaissance of Faneuil Hall and Quincy Market, handsome but dilapidated eighteenth- and nineteenth-century buildings in the historic heart of the city. He and the legendary developer Jim Rouse were visiting every bank in town, trying to raise the financing. They got nowhere. In the dozens of polite meetings, the refrain they heard from Boston's captains of industry was, "This is a nice idea, but it will never fly."

This dismal view neatly summarized the profound pessimism about Boston at that time. Boston's own business leaders turned thumbs down, not on a project in a fringe neighborhood but on Faneuil Hall and Quincy Market, landmarks in the center of the city. Fortunately, Rouse and White got the money elsewhere, and the rest is history. We are even free, from today's lofty vantage point, to pooh-pooh the shops of Faneuil Hall Marketplace as, well, somewhat tacky and touristy. But the implausible success of this project began to make a very different statement about urban possibilities.

If, in 1975, Boston's downtown was emptied out and desolate, the city's neighborhoods were a train wreck: lunar landscapes of weed-filled vacant lots, boarded-up houses, and sidewalks carpeted with broken glass. The neighborhoods had been built to house almost 800,000 people, but by 1980 were home to only about 525,000—not nearly enough to keep things up. The massive exodus between 1950 and the 1990s was the fundamental underlying reality of the so-called urban crisis—the exit of people and value.

Why did so many people leave Boston, and cities all over America, in those years? A great debate still rages about whether the process was "natural" or "induced." True, in 1950 many American cities were overcrowded, dirty, and corrupt—not seen as fit places to raise the children of the burgeoning baby-boom set off by the returning World War II veterans. And there was that Jeffersonian idea that the real America was in the country, in single-family homes with spreading lawns, leafy trees, and white picket fences.

For all that, the process was hardly "natural," or inevitable. The federal government weighed in big time—shaping the phenomenon with highways and cheap gasoline and subsidized home mortgages available only in the suburbs. The government was, throughout this period, profoundly anticity and really remains so to this day. But that makes the improbable urban comeback that is occurring all over America all the more remarkable, and a testament to the resilience of the American city.

The comeback of Boston was anything but natural—against all

odds and unforeseen. The truly wonderful thing is that it was engineered—by politicians, business leaders, and community activists who stubbornly refused to accept the apparent verdict of history on Boston. Along the way, spectacular mistakes and failures occurred; but in Boston they not only were not fatal, they were learned from.

As Jack Beatty notes in his essay, a great turn in Boston politics occurred in 1949, when the largely Irish Boston electorate turned away from the parochialism and ethnic polarization of James Michael Curley and his imitators and elected John Hynes mayor. Hynes talked of a "New Boston," embraced the largely Brahmin downtown business leadership, and launched the "urban renewal" period, which his successor John Collins brought into full flower.

\* \* \*

Urban renewal is not remembered fondly today, and its products are legitimately despised by many. In Boston, urban renewal gave us a kind of rogues' gallery of design catastrophes: Charles River Park, City Hall Plaza, and the Prudential Center—preceded by the legendary demolitions of the West End and Scollay Square neighborhoods, places that are romanticized by today's urbanists as epitomizing the wonderfully messy genius of city life.

But the facile condemnation of this era from today's vantage point of revived urbanism fails to account for the true desperation of the 1950s and 1960s, a time when Boston was dying. And urban renewal—crude, clumsy, and even antiurban though it was—at least marked an attempt to stimulate investment, to build, to do something.

Jane Holtz Kay in her essay rightly laments the tremendous self-inflicted wounds of that time, most of which have yet to heal, but it was the first, stumbling attempt to reinvent an urban future—again, against all prevailing wisdom. And in an odd way, the mistakes of the period led us to smarter strategies in the days ahead—"Let's not do that again."

If some point to the mayoral election of 1949 as a turning point, others nominate Massachusetts governor Frank Sargent's decision to cancel a major city highway project in 1970 as a truer watershed in Boston's renaissance. In the postwar era, America's love affair with the automobile had taken the form of the construction of the vast interstate highway system, which was, among other things, an act of great violence against cities. Anyone who doubts this should consult Robert Caro's epic biography of Robert Moses, *The Power Broker*. Although Moses did his work in New York, the postwar highway boom wrecked city neighborhoods everywhere, tearing the urban fabric. In fact, a major chapter in Boston's current renaissance is occupied with a conscious attempt to bind up the portions of the city riven by the earlier period of highway building.

Frank Sargent unexpectedly set Boston on a new course by abruptly canceling the so-called Boston Inner Belt. As the urban critic James Howard Kunstler says of the proposed beltway: "It was a howling super dog of a road. It would have cut clean through the neighborhoods of Hyde Park, Roxbury, Jamaica Plain, Brighton, Allston, and then across the river through Cambridge and Somerville, taking out an estimated three thousand homes.... There was some vague sense that the city was about to be gutted like a codfish."

Sargent's act reminds us that however we devalue and despise politics, the decisions of public men and women matter hugely. A part of Boston's good fortune has been to be well served by its principal politicians. After Hynes and Collins came Mayors Kevin White, Raymond Flynn, and Tom Menino. Each moved the city ahead in decisive ways, and were collective evidence of the good judgment of the Boston electorate.

Like Hynes, White (narrowly elected in 1967) was the expansive, visionary alternative to a return to the cramped, parochial past, this time in the candidacy of Louise Day Hicks. Because of Faneuil Hall Marketplace, White is remembered as a great architect of Boston's downtown and waterfront revival, but his real genius was for the neighborhoods.

*       *       *

Boston is an innovative city, with a long list of civic "firsts" on its résumé—the first public school, the first free public library, the first paid police force, and the first American subway. In his essay, Scott Kirsner dubs Boston "Innovation City," and rightly so, because this city always has been a wellspring of technological firsts—from advances in electricity to general anesthesia to robotics. Kevin White initiated his own electrifying period of innovation, including the creation of "little city halls" in every neighborhood, "community" schools—which opened new school buildings for community use into the evening hours—and neighborhood health centers, a new kind of clinic that replaced the disappearing primary care physician. Energetic and charismatic, he recruited talented aides and defiantly promoted the "livable city" as a positive ideal.

When an exhausted White left office in 1983 after four tumultuous terms, he was replaced by Ray Flynn, whose ascension to the mayor's office was both unlikely and enormously significant for the life of the city.

Flynn began his political career as a garden-variety Southie pol—a disciple of Louise Day Hicks and a fervent antidesegregation activist. Somewhere, somehow, Flynn made the decision to rise, and in so doing committed himself to building a broader constituency, which necessarily required him to modify his views. The success of his career is testament to how progress in democracies is often harnessed to the political ambitions of individuals.

＊　＊　＊

As Howard Bryant notes in his essay, race is often the asterisk in accounts of Boston's progress, and the school desegregation crisis of the 1970s is still an uncomfortable defining moment for a city struggling to move beyond it. The drama of this era is actually what first enticed me to Boston, and into the Kevin White administration. My father was a lifelong public school teacher and administrator, and as an undergraduate I had studied the role of public education in American history. I was fascinated by the desegregation struggle.

In America, we have routinely called upon our public schools to take on all of society's unsolved problems. We asked the schools to forge our democracy in the late eighteenth and early nineteenth centuries. Later, we asked them to assimilate the torrent of immigrants pouring into U.S. factories and farms. In the mid-twentieth century we asked them to win the cold war by turning out scientists, engineers, and mathematicians. And then in Boston, and in other cities, we asked them to cure the poisonous legacy of racial discrimination.

However justified the federal court finding that the Boston School Committee had systematically discriminated against black schoolchildren, which it certainly had, the remedy of school busing to achieve racial balance delivered another great body blow to a city already reeling, hemorrhaging people and vitality to the suburbs and beyond.

The middle period of Kevin White's sixteen years as mayor was thoroughly preoccupied with getting the city through the trauma. It was a scary period, in part because it licensed extremists and haters.

Anyone who was here then had their own encounters with the unleashed bigotry and violence of the time. Mine was on a snowy night in 1977. My roommate and I were settled in, watching the late TV news in our Jamaica Plain triple-decker, when we heard a frightful commotion outside . . . shouting, then screaming and crashing.

We hurtled down the stairs and out onto the street, where we interrupted four white men who were administering a merciless beating to a defenseless black man, who was covered in blood. Well, we *thought* he was defenseless. Startled by our sudden arrival, the four thugs jumped into their idling white sedan and drove off. The victim pursued his attackers, grabbing a folding chair that was "reserving" a shoveled-out parking space on the narrow street (a Boston custom) and smashing it against the rear of the car, shattering a window in the process. We all gave chase, but the car, whose driver doused the lights so we couldn't read the license plate, vanished into the night. The beaten man, a Jamaican immigrant, had lost his coat in the scuffle and his white shirt was crimson. The good news was that he was not seriously injured, even though his facial cuts had bled profusely.

My roommate and I both worked in the mayor's office, and the next day we put our "access" to work. At our behest the police department assigned a couple of detectives to the case. They shrewdly canvassed every auto glass shop in Boston, and by the end of the day they had made several arrests. It was my first experience with having some "clout" and I admit I liked it quite a lot.

But it was a terrible time, and created a great stain on Boston's reputation, which persists for many to this day. Derrick Z. Jackson's essay is a finely nuanced present accounting of the progress of race relations in the city.

* * *

I left Boston in 1985 to work in New York. This move had the added benefit of giving me an "outsider's" view of Boston's turnaround. Thirteen years later I returned, and I was stunned by the changes—almost all positive—that I saw in the city. The old tribalism seemed to have waned, leaving a forward-looking city more permeable, tolerant, and humane than the one I remembered.

One of the ways this came home to me was on an outing to Fort Independence, located on Castle Island on the tip of the South Boston peninsula, an area once known as the "Irish Riviera." By the time I returned in 1998, I had three young boys, and we went out to the island on a grand summer Sunday afternoon to wade in the shallows and watch the 747s roar over us on their way to Logan Airport.

As I watched my sons splash around and hunt for crabs, I suddenly realized that among the throngs of picnickers and strollers were a large number of African Americans enjoying the day like everyone else, looking perfectly relaxed, making the Irish Riviera their own. The city had certainly changed, and maybe it took being away for a while to recognize just how much. In an essay titled "Hooked on Boston: A Love Story," Susan Orlean describes returning to Boston, too, but in her case she discovered, with surprise and delight, how much more fun and spirited the city has become since she had left it years before.

Clearly a great deal remains to be done, but Boston has more than answered the threshold question: It has persevered through the bad old days to thrive, and more, to make a kind of statement about the good city. The good city is innovative and fun, it is prosperous, it strives for justice and sustainability—and above all, it is alive.

Beginning in the 1990s Mayor Tom Menino, a gruff contrarian who is possibly the most popular mayor in the city's history, further embroidered the "comeback." Keenly attentive to the neighborhoods, he has built new parks, revived the once moribund neighborhood commercial districts, and driven crime down to levels not seen since the early 1960s. Downtown and the waterfront have received attention, too, and the most obvious payoff has been the enormous new popularity of "downtown living"—largely affluent young professionals and so-called empty nesters moving into the heart of the city. For those of us who remember when everyone with choices seemed to be leaving, this is an extraordinary development.

Economic trends now, incredibly, favor the city. Our extraordinary constellation of colleges and universities (sixty-five in metro Boston, including eight research universities) are a rich bounty in a "knowledge economy." Largely one-third of the city's population is made up of well-educated young professionals. Boston's old economic paradigm was: Attract companies. The new economic paradigm is: Attract talent who will attract entrepreneurs and companies. Lawrence Summers, the formidable president of Harvard since 2001, forecasts that Boston can be the epicenter of the coming life-sciences explosion.

This invigoration of city life extends to every aspect. Dining out—perhaps the quintessential and most democratic expression of urbanity—has been transformed. In 1980 there was only one romantic restaurant in Boston, Café Budapest, and two others where you could have a serious meal, the venerable Locke-Ober near Downtown Crossing, or the dining room of the Ritz on Arlington Street. The 2004 Zagat guide to Boston restaurants is a stunning extravaganza of diverse culinary delights. With nationally renowned chefs like Todd English and Lydia Shire and top-notch restaurants like L'Espalier, Via Matta, and Lala Rokh, Boston has now taken its place as one of the premier eating-out towns, along with New York, Philadelphia, Chicago, and Los Angeles.

What's wrong with this picture? Well, there are big problems; but from any relative perspective they are the problems we want to have. Two of the biggest are directly traceable to Boston's vigorous good health. First is the horrific cost of housing; second is the issue of managing well all the development that wants to happen in Boston.

Affordable housing didn't used to be such an issue. Boston was declining so rapidly that there was all sorts of affordable housing (admittedly much of it substandard). But the new popularity of the city, combined with the trend toward smaller households, has triggered tremendous price appreciation in both rental and ownership properties. The average—yes, average—price of a single-family home in metro Boston is now close to $350,000.

In their essays, both Lynda Morgenroth and Michael Patrick Mac-Donald address the negative effects of the rising price of real estate. When artists and writers like Morgenroth are driven out to the more affordable suburbs, the city is robbed of their unique perspective. MacDonald is concerned about the gentrification of some of Boston's older neighborhoods, which can result in denying the children of longtime residents the option of living in the places where they grew up.

The city proper, under Menino's leadership, actually produces a great deal of housing. Boston's vaunted community development corporations, or CDCs, are neighborhood-based housing producers that are among the best in the nation. CDCs have helped to build some twenty thousand units of affordable housing in Boston over the last twenty years.

But the suburbs are not participating. Through a variety of time-tested means, most notably large-lot zoning, most communities outside Boston actively repel the creation of any apartments or single-family homes on small lots. This lack of production drives prices up and sprawl outward—simultaneously diffusing the energy of the urban core and further destroying the rural landscape. If the housing problem is not addressed—and it will take a regional solution—the economy could founder as skilled young people exit for more affordable locales, as is already occurring to some degree.

As to development, there are at least four major, city-shaping processes simultaneously under way, each of which rivals the creation of the Back Bay in their potential historical significance. The magnitude of all this is so great as to raise fears about whether the community, through its agencies, can properly oversee it all—and, of course, infuse it with the crucial pro-urban values underlying the city's recovery.

I speak of course of the fabled "Big Dig," now completed as a road project and quickly morphing into a park design project; the larger question of the waterfront, really in the infancy of its build out; the development of the "air rights" over the in-city portion of the Massachusetts Turnpike; and finally, Harvard University's intention to build a mammoth second campus in Allston across the river from its ancestral Cambridge home.

This is all very exciting, and represents prospects that nearly every American city envies. Yet there are hazards. Principal among them is the lack of clear authority and accountability. Jurisdictional ambiguity and conflict between city and state government and their disputatious progeny of special-purpose authorities pervades every one of these undertakings. One of the legacies of earlier chapters of Boston's ethnic conflict is that the city of Boston has less "home rule" than other major cities. State government intrudes deeply into city affairs, which makes each project a venue for the de novo negotiation of just who is in charge.

Sometimes the negotiations do not produce a satisfactory resolution. For instance, it was envisioned that by this stage of the Big Dig project, the state and the city would have created a special-purpose entity that would design and manage the extraordinary new twenty-seven-acre park to be created above the sunken highway. But political impasse persists; with the result that by default, the Massachusetts Turnpike Authority is overseeing the preliminary design of the park. Insane, but that's Boston; and we can only hope that the state and the city have more successful parleys about the other major developments under way.

The saving grace will be that the politicians will not be left entirely to their own devices. As important as our politicians are, all of their decisions will be influenced, modified, and occasionally overturned by Boston's truly distinctive asset—the vast web of private individuals and groups passionately active in city life. Boston birthed the abolitionist movement in the nineteenth century, and it has bred a special brand of impatient activism ever since.

These are the activists who dreamed of a New Boston with John Hynes, these are the citizens of Boston who stopped the highway with Frank Sargent, who staffed Kevin White's little city halls and community schools, who transformed race relations with Ray Flynn and combated youth violence with Tom Menino.

Do you want to know why I'm an optimist about Boston? Because that activism is an inexhaustible resource. It will guide us—and save us—in the very interesting days ahead.

# Hooked on Boston:
# A Love Story

*Susan Orlean*

I didn't think I'd be coming back to Boston after my first stint living here, but then I fell in love—hook, line, and sinker—with a Bostonian and got reeled back in, a happy fish but a hesitant one. I had first lived in the city a million years ago, long before I met this alluring Bostonian who brought me back. I had come in a hurry and left in a hurry, surprised by the traffic (tangled), the food (excuse me, boiled dinner??), and mostly the character of the place. Boston seemed to me a little old-maidish: stubborn, stolid, and frumpy, and quite proud of its stubborn, stolid frumpiness. More than that, the city seemed inclined to finger-wag at anything frisky, nimble, and chic. Oh, how Boston and I rubbed each other the wrong way! I felt all thumbs here, too loudly eager for excitement and ambition and eccentricity. Old maids do not go for clamorous, ambitious excitement-seekers. I finally decided that we—the city and I—were not a good match, so I decamped to New York. I loved New York to pieces, and figured I would not be likely to ever again have an address in Somerville or Back Bay.

But then, as I said, I fell in love. This is not the occasion for going into details on the particulars, but I would like to say here that I was misled into believing that this fellow, with whom I had fallen in love, lived in New York. I really was. He claims that misleading me was not intentional, although he knew when we met that I was pretty well rooted in New York and might not survive being replanted in the Boston bean pot. But the truth, eventually, was revealed. I figured out why his New York address was strangely similar to that of the New York Hilton, and that was that. He confessed that he lived on Beacon Hill and that his New York visits were, indeed, just visits. But by then it was too late to call the whole thing off, because we were crazy about each other. We courted for the next six months along the I-95 corridor and then made it official with a nice wedding in the 10011 zip code. Then we determined that marriage might be a good time to start living together. He couldn't move because of his job, but I could, so I boxed up my belongings and came back to Boston.

Here's what it has been like. You know how you feel at your high school reunion? That you've gotten better but everyone else has gotten older and fatter and balder? That's what I was bracing myself for. I'd been gone almost fourteen years, and I prided myself on having gotten, during that time, livelier and more adventurous, but I expected Boston to be fourteen years older and more unbending and more proper. For once in my life, I was very happy to be wrong. In the years since I left, the city has managed some magical reversal of time: It's gotten younger, more agile, and refreshed. Buildings have gone up; the Central Artery has gone down. The dustiest parts of downtown have been brushed off and repopulated. Neighborhoods like South Boston that had been stopped up and ingrown have a new pep imparted by the new people crisscrossing them, discovering their characters, making them home.

What matters most, and what I like the most, is that the city doesn't feel hidebound anymore. Of course, Boston will always be bookish. That is one of its wonders. But being bookish and smart, which is what the Boston of the moment feels like to me, is not the same as being a crabby librarian, which is what it used to feel like. Let Miami be the tannest city, and Chicago the most mercantile; let Los

Angeles be the most glamorous, and let New York be—well, New York. Boston is, and should revel in being, the brainiest American city. That's how it strikes me now, rather than how it used to feel, when it seemed to be the squarest and the most entrenched.

I live in a neighborhood that hardly existed when I was last here. It is way downtown, across a little inlet of water called Fort Point Channel. The neighborhood comprises a bunch of square-shouldered old brick warehouses and factories and small turn-of-the-century office buildings. The businesses left long ago, except for a few joke-supply shops and model-shipbuilders and a lobster outlet or two, and when Boston was in its doldrums, the rest of the buildings were abandoned to molder and collapse. Then artists colonized them, taking advantage of the lovely openness of the spaces within the old warehouses, and, even better, the perfect view the neighborhood has of the city skyline, the sunset, and boats puttering by in the then dirty but now scrubbed clean Boston Harbor. I'm part of the third wave of residents down here: I'm not a joke merchant, a lobsterman, or a visual artist; I'm just someone who likes the crazy overlay of industrial remnants and downtown boogie-woogie and the thick texture of an urban area. There is a lot that's new down here, and that's the point, but there is also a lot that's old, which is the other point and the more critical one. Boston is not, thank goodness, Fort Lauderdale, where everything looks like it was just unwrapped and taken out of the box. The new development here—the Raphael Vinoly–designed Convention and Exhibition Center, the gorgeous federal courthouse, the Channel Center residential blocks, the cool, glassy-skinned Manulife headquarters—is jumbled in with the great old Boston stalwarts like fish warehouses, banks, triple-deckers, and Irish bars. It's a nice, salty mix, and when I jog around my neighborhood on those mornings when I'm not too lazy, I love the way I can pass several different centuries and economies and atmospheres in one not-too-ambitious run.

My husband likes to think he is the smartest man in the world. He thinks this for many reasons, but one is that he made a case to me that Boston now is not what I remembered of Boston then, that I would find a new and different place from the one I knew a little bit long ago; that it is looser, faster, funnier, and more fun. He's right—not about being the smartest man in the world, although he is a very serious contender—but about everything he claimed about the city. It's almost more thrilling to have not discovered Boston but to have rediscovered it, especially at this moment when it has broken through the last bit of crust that had made it, in the past, somewhat harder to love. I will never drop the *r* in "park" or quite understand the appeal of a boiled dinner, but I am happy to say I'm hooked.

# An Eden of Sorts:
# An Unnatural History
# of the Shawmut Peninsula

*John Hanson Mitchell*

I grew up in a household that upheld the clipper ship as
some sort of hallowed icon and the shipbuilder Donald McKay as an
earthly version of the archangel. I was the youngest by many years in
a family of five and barely able to comprehend what was meant by all
this, but I did manage to understand that clipper ships were ranked
somewhere between heaven and earth, that they were fast, that they
sailed the seven seas, and that they emanated from a place called
Boston.

Periodically, my father would take down from the shelf the verita-
ble bible of these matters, Samuel Eliot Morison's *Maritime History
of Massachusetts, 1783–1860,* and read, as from a sacred text, of the arrival
of a clipper ship in Boston Harbor after a voyage around the world:
"A summer day with the scent of new cut hay on the salt air and a
full-rigged ship, slowly emerging from Massachusetts Bay, sailing
past Boston Light, then hauling a few points on the wind to shoot
the Narrows between Georges, Gallops, and Lovells Islands, and
then paying off again through President Road, and finally booming

up the stream past the Castle, where lounging soldiers, out for a breath of sea air, would be struck dumb with the beauty of it all."

My father would close the book solemnly at this point and there would be a devout silence around the table. Over the mantle, like the Madonna of more traditional households, we had an oil painting of Donald McKay's ship *Flying Cloud*, running before the wind—all sails set, of course. I seem to remember my father bowing toward it after the reading. But that is probably my imagination.

\* \* \*

These days, flying low into Logan Airport in the late afternoon when the light is raking and the shadows are long, you cannot help but be impressed with the fact that Boston is a port city, characterized by the contrast of the high cliff faces of its newer buildings with an ironic scattering of unpopulated islands that dot the scalloped harbor. These islands are the result of geological forces; specifically, the work of the last glacial advance that overspread New England some sixty thousand years ago. As the ice retreated, along with the islands, it left behind a little tadpole-shaped headland, its tail attached to the American continent and its head pointing seaward. The place, long known to Native Americans, was marked on early European maps as the Shawmut Peninsula.

One September afternoon a few years ago, returning to the city on one of the little ferries that run out to the islands, I saw what appeared to be a fifteenth-century sailing vessel plugging along under full sail, with the towers of the Boston skyline rising in the background and low-flying jets roaring overhead. It turned out to be a replica of John Cabot's brave little vessel, the *Matthew*, on her way home from a transatlantic passage undertaken to celebrate the five hundredth anniversary of Cabot's 1497 exploration of the New England coast.

Cabot landed somewhere along these shores and described a rich land of fruit trees and berry bushes, an account filled out in later years by imaginative chroniclers who also put in here. The tight little island that would become Boston was alive with strawberries, whortleberries, larch, birch, witch hazel, and beech. There were wild turkeys, martens, strange animals with flattened tails called beavers, and other marvelous creatures, including the "strong-armed beare, large-limmed Mooses, and the tripping Deere," to quote one source. Never mind that these early explorers also encountered here the "Kingly Lyon" and Tritons, and peppered their maps with images of sea serpents and mermaids; the place was an Eden of sorts, "The Paradise of all these parts," as the explorer Captain John Smith wrote in his 1616 mapping of the region.

The first permanent European resident of the Shawmut Peninsula was an Anglican clergyman named William Blackstone, who settled on Beacon Hill in 1625. He was a slightly eccentric gentleman, the first of many who seemed to favor this place, who lived alone in his English thatched cottage, with his cow, his herd of pigs, a vegetable garden, and another enduring characteristic of the site, a library of more than 150 books. Five years later the ship *Arbella* landed with a company of Puritan settlers under the leadership of John Winthrop. At Blackstone's invitation, Winthrop and his Puritans established a colony on the peninsula and renamed the place Boston.

\* \* \*

For the first fifteen thousand years of its existence, the peninsula was characterized by sharp little hills—Copps Hill, Fort Hill, Dorchester Heights, and of course Beacon Hill, the largest of them all. But unlike Blackstone, who chose to live with nature rather than contrary to it, the Puritans began to remake the place. They cleared the forests of the oaks and hickories that once supported Blackstone's herd of swine. They constructed lanes, then streets, then a "Great Highwaye to Roxberre." They built docks, ferry landings, windmills, and meetinghouses, and when they were done with that they leveled the hills and used the fill to widen the tail of the tadpole to create more dry land. With these activities, John Winthrop and company began a process of leveling and filling and digging and delving in Boston that is still going on today.

Deep history notwithstanding, the story of the natural world of Boston is not so much what once was (after all, every place was better in the folklore of things) as what it will be in the future. There has been an evolution of the attitudes in this city that has caused the natural elements of the peninsula to rise and fall according to the whims of its human inhabitants. One of the great ironies of the town is that it was founded by a pious citizenry that believed fervently that ye cannot serve both God and mammon—and then spent the next two hundred years working assiduously for mammon. Then, once they had made their money, the old ethic reasserted itself and in the mid-nineteenth century, the descendants of the Puritan families began to throw bad money after good. They built libraries and museums, schools for the deaf and the blind; they saw to the welfare of animals, established a symphony orchestra, and, of course, spent an inordinate amount of their money on educational institutions. They also built green parks—some five thousand acres, all told—and, unintentionally perhaps, launched a campaign that eventually created the American environmental movement.

I was once asked to deliver a lecture to a remnant of this old order of Boston society, the estimable ladies of the Beacon Hill Garden Club, an institution, which among other benevolent social accomplishments, serves as the guardian of the hidden gardens of Beacon Hill, small private sanctuaries that are open to the public on one day a year. I had been out of town just before the event and had to plan my talk at the last minute on my way across Boston Common.

This was November; the leaves were off the trees, but the grass of the Common was still green, and it occurred to me that I might as well do a show-and-tell for the good women of Beacon Hill, so I began looking for edible wild plants. Immediately I found a black walnut. Then I found a butternut hickory, then the acorns of three different species of oaks. Perfect, I thought. I could spend an easy twenty minutes discussing the Native Americans' use of mast, in particular their use of acorns—how they would gather them and then boil them by dropping fire-heated rocks into pots, and how, after this process, they would roast them and grind them into a meal. That could lead into a fuller discussion of Native American food plants of Beacon Hill before it was Beacon Hill and still covered with wild oak and hickory and perhaps barrens of blueberries and huckleberries.

Not ten yards farther along I spotted a dandelion. Here was another story—favorite edible wild plant of southern Europeans who settled in the North End and used the fresh leaves of spring for greens. In among the dandelions, I found the leaf of a plant in the amaranth family, one of the most commonly used native plants of the Americas, a staple food crop of the Incas and a plant that is currently coming back into fashion as a grain among the health conscious of this world. Then, in an as yet unmulched old flower bed, I saw what I believed to be the leaf of a young pokeweed, then another dandelion and a healthy growth of purslane. Growing in among these delicious and sadly overlooked potherbs I saw what I took to be a young honey mushroom. I snatched it up. Another twenty minutes on the glories of mycology: the delicious family of boletes, fields and lawns of succulent *Agaricus campestris,* chanterelles, oyster mushrooms, and then the dark side, the poisonous destroying angel.

At the top of the hill I stood and looked back across the Common. This is, if any place is, central city, the heart of Boston, and yet all I could see were the November trees and the green sweep of autumn lawns, complete with strollers, runners, sleepers, and daydreamers. With my collection of edible plants in hand, I started thinking about the fact that this natural place was the common ground of this uncommon city and that, as residents of this Hill, the honorable ladies of the Garden Club still had rights to graze their cows on this common—if, perchance, any of them had cows.

If you walk up Beacon Hill, cross over the top, and head down the west side, you come in due time to another defining characteristic of this coastal town, the great artery that is the river Charles. Like most urban rivers the Charles went into a sad decline with the advent of the industrial revolution. It was originally a narrow winding stream that curved in and around the cities of Cambridge and Boston, with wide tidal flats on either side that provided a nutrient-rich environment for uncounted numbers of shellfish, sandworms, bloodworms, and migratory fish such as shad and alewife, and in the lower reaches, oysters and mussels and huge, twenty-five-pound lobsters, which in better times the resident bears would snatch from between the rocks. Even into the nineteenth century, early photographs of the tidal flats, taken at low tide, reveal clam diggers bent over the glistening banks. Generally, though, by the 1850s, with the expanded population, what had been a valued resource became a plague. The flats had accumulated so much sewage and offal from the housing and slaughter-houses and fisheries that lined its banks, it had become a stinking quagmire that infected the city twice a day at low tide.

As the end of the century approached, many public officials and private citizens began to lobby to have the river and its banks transformed from a health hazard into an environment that would contribute to the fitness and pleasure of the population. One of the prime movers in this effort was Charles Eliot, who worked for the landscape firm of Fredrick Law Olmsted and was of the belief that all those who value natural beauty should band together to preserve something of the native environment for the people of the city.

The result, with some adjustments, was a linear "water park," an open green space with promenades and walkways that extended for nine miles along both banks of the river. In order to halt the natural flow of the tides and keep the stinking flats permanently drowned, the plans called for a dam near the mouth of the river at the base of Beacon Hill. There was a little flurry of objection from a few of the Brahmins who had property overlooking the river and worried—somewhat uncharacteristically—about the impoverished Irish who used to dig clams on the flats. But by 1910 the dam was built and by 1930, thanks to a generous donation from Helen Storrow, the widow of one of the major backers of the project, James Jackson Storrow, the park was finally completed. There was a twist, however. The one condition of Mrs. Storrow's gift, stated in her will, was that no road ever be constructed through the new park. Soon after Helen Storrow's death in 1949, the state legislature voted to construct a highway along the river—and named their blasphemy Storrow Drive.

The Charles River park is (or used to be) termed Boston's "Central Park" by urban watchers, and is considered one of the major public green spaces of any city in the United States. But it is rivaled by another Olmsted-designed Boston park, the fabled Emerald Necklace.

*   *   *

The idea for a rural park for the city began just after the Civil War, which were bright years of city planning, both in the United States and England. During the late nineteenth century, there was an emerging social conscience that held that the one great benefit for the struggling working classes, trapped as they were in squalid tenements, was access to space, air, and light. Although Olmsted didn't think of it that way, his intention was to reverse many of the clearances started by the Puritans and bring the country into the city to create an environment in which the people could stroll and breathe freely. He proposed a continuous seven-mile park that would begin at the Common and the Public Gardens and then flow down Commonwealth Avenue along a tree-lined esplanade to the Back Bay Fens. From here it would follow the course of the somewhat misnamed Muddy River, upstream through marshes of the Fens to Jamaica Pond and along a strip known as the Arborway to the Arnold Arboretum and Franklin Park, and on to end at another park and promenade at Castle Island on the harbor, where the tired workers could stroll of a Sunday afternoon and benefit from the salutary effects of sea breezes.

Each spring and fall this landscape of trees and shrubs, interwoven with meadows, community gardens, ponds and streams, and freshwater marshes in the midst of an urban setting, now attracts to its thickets and pools any number of resident birds, as well as flocks of migratory land birds. This green skein, woven through a world of steel and concrete and brick and glass, harbors wildlife such as raccoons and opossums, snakes, and, of course, squirrels. There are also sections in this system, mainly in the Arnold Arboretum, with its diverse collection of flowering trees and shrubs, where, with a little imagination, you might think for a minute that you have somehow been transported to the shadowed glens of the European countryside. The deception is intentional, of course, and the fact that it works is a credit to the designers.

As far as the illusion of wildness, though, the best spot in Boston, apart maybe from the outer islands of the harbor, can be found in Franklin Park in the wide, semiwild part of the park that Olmsted aptly named "the Wilderness," an eighty-acre section of native oaks and hickories and shaded dells of hemlock. Olmsted's intention here was to leave a representative model of the primal landscape of the Shawmut Peninsula that William Blackstone and the first Puritan settlers would have known, and except for the invasion of a number of alien species of plants, such as the beds of periwinkles that overspread the hollows, he more or less succeeded. But from the top of the hill in the Wilderness you can get a good view across the city to a wilder place, the Blue Hills Reservation, which lies to the south. Unlike Olmsted's invented wilderness, this park still contains much of the native flora and fauna of the region in its natural state, including a number of nesting raptors and the endangered timber rattlesnake.

Olmsted and Eliot's greened version of Boston owes a lot to Europe. The large freshwater lake created by the damming of the Charles was based directly on Alster Park in Hamburg, Germany, and Franklin Park is, in effect, a transplanted bit of Old England. Many of Olmsted's and Eliot's ideas evolved from the design work of the English garden planner Capability Brown, who favored wide sweeping vistas, ponds, and wooded bosks. As the natural city reemerged from the built environment of the past, the old primitive energies of wild nature reasserted themselves. You can sometimes experience this in the most unlikely places.

A few years ago, residents of the fashionable Back Bay were entertained over a period of weeks when a saw-whet owl took up a hunting station in a garbage alley in back of their apartments. Formerly endangered peregrine falcons now nest on the high cliffs of a few of the city's skyscrapers, supporting themselves by feeding on the resident pigeons. A year or so back, passing through the Fenway, my daughter saw one hit a pigeon full force. That same year, in the nearby Mount Auburn Cemetery, another famous Boston natural landmark (which technically belongs to Cambridge, across the river), I saw a red-tailed hawk blast a squirrel out of an oak tree and proceed to tear it apart in front of a group of only moderately shocked tourists. The rarely seen, but extremely common, little brown snake can be found even in the saw-whet-haunted alleys of Back Bay. Raccoons, opossums, and the occasional coyote appear from time to time in the city. Belle Isle Marsh, the last wild salt marsh in Boston, has large flocks of herons and egrets, a population of snowy owls in winter, garter snakes, flocks of shorebirds in summer, and marsh hawks, as well as the usual assembly of muskrats, raccoons, and opossums, which seem to be common through the city.

*   *   *

The Emerald Necklace is hardly the only public green space in Boston. Interspersed with the city's historical squares and cultural monuments are community gardens and public gardens, ponds and lakes, and moldering graveyards rich with history, ocean parks, river ways, bird trails, and, once you get off onto the harbor islands, even campgrounds. Most of these are well known, some are new and have yet to be appreciated, save by their neighbors, and some have deep but little-recognized histories. One of these latter is a small suburban-style pond in what is now Brookline, called Hall's Pond.

In the late nineteenth century a woman named Minna Hall lived at Hall's Pond (no surprises here, the pond was named for her family). Minna and a good friend, her cousin Harriet Hemenway, would often walk around the shores of the pond looking for songbirds and noting their observations in their diaries and journals. On one of these walks, Harriet Hemenway began telling Minna of a horrendous article she had read about the slaughter of marsh birds in Florida. The article included graphic descriptions of the young birds, dead and dying in their nests, the parents having been killed for their plumes.

Fashions of the late nineteenth century required the addition of feathers on the large, wide-brimmed, and increasingly cumbersome decorative hats that women wore. By 1896 this fad had become ever more excessive, with vast sweeping plumes taken from the nuptial feathers of herons and egrets as well as the addition of entire birds —generally terns—their wings half open and sweeping across a woman's forehead in apparent flight. The collection of these birds and feathers created a full-scale trade for hunters, especially in the marshes of the American South, where the herons and egrets gathered in huge, noisy rookeries. The decline in bird populations was confounded by the fact that the hunters were seeking the ornate white plumes that these birds develop in spring, during the mating season. Hunters would enter a rookery, shoot the adults for their feathers, and leave whole nests of young to starve to death. Populations dropped dramatically, a fact that few noticed or perhaps even cared about, save for ornithologists.

Harriet Hemenway and Minna Hall were both daughters of Boston's Brahmin class. One of the characteristics of the female of this class was a burning social and reformist attitude. For all their supposed cold roast personalities, Brahmin women were fiery in citizenship; they were pioneers of the abolition movement, of feminism, women's literature, women's art, and settlement houses, as well as in the creation of museums and libraries. Given their lineage, Harriet and Minna determined to do something about the slaughter of the innocents that was taking place in the marshes of the Americas. They went home and ticked off the names of all their friends in the blue book, the social register of Boston, and then invited them to a tea party at Harriet Hemenway's house on Clarendon Street. Here, over Lapsang souchong tea and petits fours they described the wanton slaughter and proposed, in effect, a boycott of hats bearing the feathers of wild birds.

The tea party was a great success. Women signed on enthusiastically, and so in order to expand the boycott, Harriet and Minna proposed forming an organization, which they called the Massachusetts Audubon Society. The intention was not to limit the organization to one state, however. This was to be a national, even international, cause from the beginning. By the third meeting the board resolved to use every effort to establish similar organizations in other parts of the country, and within the year, using seed money from the Boston group, five other states from New York to Colorado had joined the cause. By 1905, the group had increased its membership substantially and went on to create a national Audubon Society.

Their little war was fought on two fronts. Women eventually killed the market for plumes through social pressure, and in 1900 Congress passed a law that prohibited the interstate shipment of animals killed in violation of state laws. By 1918, the United States passed the Migratory Bird Treaty Act, which prohibited outright the trade in feathers.

The fight wasn't over, though. There was a line in the original charter of the Boston group that said something about further protection of native birds. Birds need habitats in which to nest, and so the founding mothers began saving open space in and around Boston. The fact that nature knows no political boundaries soon became apparent as a result of their battles, and within a few decades of Harriet Hemenway's death in 1960 (she lived to be 102 and never gave up the fight), American environmental organizations were working with Canada and Central American countries to establish preserves for neotropical migratory birds.

Boston always was a bird-loving city. One of the favorite pastimes of the Brahmins was a weekend outing in the parks with opera glasses to do a bit of bird spotting. In the 1950s, these bird spotters began to notice, once more, dead and dying birds, this time as the result of pesticide poisoning. Bostonians were also bird listers, and their lists documenting a steady decline in local songbird populations impressed one woman in particular, the writer Rachel Carson. After years of deliberation and introspection as to what she was about to beget, Carson published *Silent Spring,* the seminal work that launched the modern American environmental movement. Needless to say, perhaps, for this book, Carson chose a Boston-based publisher, Houghton Mifflin.

\* \* \*

Although there are many pendants of green space dangling southward toward the great wild gem of Boston's Blue Hills Reservation to the south, Olmsted's grand design for a ring of green around the central city never really reached the sea at the southeastern end. But the open spaces appear again at the theoretical end of the necklace at Marine Park. Although slightly altered from Olmsted's original plans for the park, a footbridge runs out to Castle Island, the site of Fort Independence, and as Olmsted had hoped, the old fort and its grounds have become a favorite walking place for those dwellers of the hemmed-in streets of the inner city. Here, on any pleasant day in almost any season, are walkers, cyclists, sightseers, and dreamers.

Out beyond the ramparts, in the wide harbor, lie the island drumlins left by the glacier. These ten-thousand-year-old landforms have been much abused in the 350-plus years since the European sojourn in this coastal region began. During this era, the islands have been used as dumping grounds for both people and material. There were landfills on the islands, paupers' graveyards, mental institutions, prisons, military installations, quarantine hospitals, and, in one of the most shameful chapters in Boston history, even an early version of a concentration camp. During King Philip's War, Christianized Indians were imprisoned on Deer Island, where they died of cold and starvation. But history is fickle. Although the city attempted to obliterate the sad history of the Deer Island concentration camp by turning the island into a sewage-treatment plant, in our time, things are getting better. The dumps on the islands have been buried and capped, vegetation has returned, forts have fallen into decay, and the islands have been restored as parks under the National Park Service.

Out there, on the harbor islands, in the outlying externalities of the city, you can still get a sense of what this little cut in the coast must have been like in those early years when the *Arbella* and the *Matthew* plodded in from their transatlantic crossings. Predatory birds in the form of great horned owls, kestrels, merlins, sharp-shinned hawks, and, in winter, snowy owls, hunt the rocky landscape. Ospreys, glossy ibis, loons, herons, snow geese, brant, sea ducks such as the bufflehead, and many species of sparrows can still be found around the place that was once Wood Island, now better known as Logan Airport. Seals haul out on these shores, land mammals such as foxes, coyotes, and muskrats are common, and Grape Island, which has a popular camping area, is fast becoming notorious for its population of skunks.

Above all, though, the defining natural characteristic of Boston is not the exotic plants and animals, or the history, or even the occasionally exotic people. The overwhelming force of the place is the ever present sea; you can see it from certain sections, even between the canyon walls of the modern city, and no matter where you are, you can smell it whenever the wind is in an easterly quarter. Out on the harbor islands, on almost any day, you can experience a sensation close to that of wilderness. To know this you have but to get out to the Graves or one of the Brewster islands, and then make your way over the rocks and sit looking east. You have a whole continent behind you, and a world before you.

To the west lies the city, with its vastly reordered and now re-borning environment—a place that was created according to models developed over a hundred generations on the European continent that the settlers left behind. Today, the old native Shawmut wildness, buried for all those years by the energetic works of the Puritans—and all the immigrants who followed—is reasserting itself into the re-structured world that they created. But the work is hardly over.

This is an age with a much better understanding of the ecological complexities that make up a living city. Although they did not know what was to come, Olmsted and Eliot had the right idea in their at-tempt to create an integrated environment in which people would have access to all the advantages of the city, as well as the salutary and even spiritual benefits of nature. But what began well enough in the 1850s was dismantled in the 1950s by the blind devotion of city plan-ners to a singularly destructive invention, a machine that has undone even the best designed and most pleasant cities—the automobile.

If there is one thing that we could do to give this, and other cities, a sensible future, it would be to banish, expel, deport, and forever exile this noxious device and all its associated poisons. Boston is still a contained city; you can walk anywhere in the town in the space of an hour, and jitneys, trolleys, subways, buses, and a few taxis could carry those who can't or won't walk. Banning cars is hardly an outra-geous idea. Many European cities have already excluded automobiles from their historic centers—and seen business increase in the car-free districts. The same thing is true wherever streets are closed for pedes-trians. To my knowledge, no one has ever attempted a citywide ban of the private automobile, but given the moral foundation of the shining city on a hill, Boston would be a good place to begin.

If you want a taste of this new city, go out to the harbor islands, where there are no cars. There are days there, when the wind is right, when it seems that anything is possible. And if you happen to fall into a reverie on one of those days, who can blame you if you think you catch a hint of the smell of fresh-cut hay, and somewhere out in the mists you spot a crowd of sail just off Roaring Bulls shoals, and you hear the clank of buoys and the faint whisper of a sea chantey. And as you squint seaward, the tide rises, the east wind picks up, and the *Flying Cloud* sweeps in toward the Narrows, on her way back from a three-year round-the-world voyage, carrying with her a cargo of sandalwood from Hawaii, wine from Madeira, grapes and oranges from Spain, silk and porcelain and strong black tea from China.

No wonder the inventors of this city thought that the place was the Hub.

# A Racial Lab for the Twenty-first Century

*Derrick Z. Jackson*

In the winter of 1988–89, just after I joined the *Boston Globe,* I spoke at Roxbury Community College, the junior college spawned by the community activism of the 1960s. I told the audience that I came from *Newsday* in New York. This provoked a question from a student: Why'd you leave New York to come here?

I asked back, What do you mean?
He said, You know what I mean.
I said, Could you spell it out for me?
He said, Why'd you come here when this is the most racist city in the country?
I asked, Why do you think so?
He said, Black folks can't get anywhere in this city.

I told the young man about a favorite uncle of mine who once told me that if you do not wake up optimistic, you might as well roll back over and stay in bed. I added, I've been called *nigger* in every city I've lived in, Milwaukee, Kansas City, New York, and here. So I don't waste time deciding which city is more racist. The real question is doing your best to get somewhere, wherever you are at.

Ironically, the student spoke from the halls of an institution that was built on the backs of the black and Latino struggle in Boston. The college's brand-new campus on fifty-two acres was designed by African American architects Stull and Lee. (African American architects make up only 1.5 percent of all the architects in the United States.) Yet the roadblock was in the student's mind. Black folks can't get anywhere.

That makes Boston as important a racial laboratory of the twenty-first century as there is in the nation. Because of the busing violence of the 1970s, immortalized by the gang of white men who used an American flag on a pole to spear a black man, no city north of the Mason-Dixon line is viewed as more racist. When I left *Newsday* for the *Globe,* several of my New York City journalism colleagues gave me last rites at a bar.

The continuing roadblocks made Hubie Jones, a former Boston University dean and a special assistant to the chancellor for urban affairs at the University of Massachusetts, Boston, say in a 2001 *Boston Globe* feature, "Virulent racism permeates all levels and aspects of political, economic and social life in the city."

This is also a city with an impressive legion of African Americans who are undeterred by the past and determined to transform barriers into brick and mortar for opportunity. This is a city that might surprise you with how so many people of color pursue crafts and careers with unbridled optimism. The same Hubie Jones—who has spent decades fighting for justice in community development and has been a savior-at-large in countless arenas and who minced no words about the barriers—also said, in 1996, "I'm here because I love this town, economically, culturally, educationally, it's great. But we have this abnormal nonparticipation of blacks in the social fabric of the city. Things are improving, but we're not there yet. So I have a lovers' quarrel with Boston."

* * *

It is a lovers' quarrel because of many of the negative head-lines of the early 1990s.

There was the Charles Stuart murder case, in which a white man killed his pregnant wife, then shot himself, then blamed it all on a black man. City Hall set the police loose on African American men with a stop-and-frisk campaign that strayed far from the original descriptions of the alleged assailant. What was particularly revealing were the first few days in January 1990, after Stuart's story was exposed as a hoax and he committed suicide. Mayor Ray Flynn called for a community healing service at Mission Church. The church was only a few football fields away from the Mission Hill projects, where the black people most affected by the sweeps lived.

But the church, up on a hill and filled with Eurocentric icons and paintings, symbolically was not a place for healing. About a thousand people came, but by my estimate, 85 to 90 percent of the people were white. Of the leaders at the altar, only one was African American. A black woman at the healing service, Elaine Sutherland, was so angry she said, "This was garbage." Down in the projects, Hattie Dudley, head of the Mission Extension Task Force, said that night, "We are not ready to be healed. No one has spoken to us. The mayor has not spoken to us. The black leadership has spoken for us, but most of them have not spoken to us, either."

City leaders again called for healing in 1994 after police mistakenly raided the home of a seventy-five-year-old retired minister, Accelyne Williams. Police chased Williams, forced him to the floor, and handcuffed him. Williams vomited and died of a heart attack.

Even though white students are disporportionately represented at Boston Latin public high school, a white father angry that his daughter was unfairly passed over by less qualified students of color filed suit and single-handedly destroyed affirmative action there by 1998. In 2001 real estate redlining was still alive. A 2003 *Boston Globe* study found that male drivers of color were far more likely to be ticketed for speeding than white drivers.

In the fall of 2003 two Boston talk show hosts, joking about a gorilla that escaped from the Franklin Park Zoo, a zoo surrounded by black and Latino neighborhoods, called the animal a Metco gorilla trying to escape to Lexington. Metco is the voluntary program where African American students fleeing the Boston Public Schools travel to suburban districts. The zoo itself is symbolic, as Boston has the strange status of having one mediocre zoo in the suburbs and one mediocre one in the city, clearly dividing resources that would be better spent on one sparkling facility.

That incident came on the heels of a debacle in which a five-year-old black student and resident of Wellesley, an affluent and predominately white suburb, was put on a Metco bus back to Boston. That incident brought back echoes of 1990, when Wellesley police, saying they were looking for a black man who robbed a bank, drew guns on the Boston Celtics' Dee Brown and handcuffed him facedown on the ground. Brown had just purchased a $750,000 home in Wellesley.

You could go on and on. But then, one has to halt, get a grip, and say, is Boston all that different from the rest of America? After all, despite the legend that Atlanta is a black mecca, didn't African American midlevel managers sue Coca-Cola over its glass ceilings? The nation's most publicized cases of police brutality in the 1990s came from New York and Los Angeles. The most notorious cases of police profiling came from New Jersey and Maryland. Cities like Milwaukee, Detroit, Cleveland, and St. Louis were all rated as more segregated than Boston in 2002 by the U.S. Census data.

Those who want to argue that Boston is different have some ammunition. While 45 percent of African Americans and Latinos live in suburbs in the United States, the percentage of black and brown people who live in Boston's suburbs is only 25 percent, according to researchers at the State University of New York at Albany. In the city itself, Boston has one of the nation's highest levels of white flight from the public schools. White children make up 25 percent of Boston's youths under eighteen. But they are only 14 percent of its elementary school students.

Then there is the bugaboo about political leadership. Boston is among the last of the nation's big cities never to have had a mayor of color. The possible reasons are heavily debated, from old-boy white networks that solidified their patronage after the serious 1983 mayoral run of African American Mel King to apathy from voters of color and disorganization among potential candidates.

Those networks were apparent when Mayor Thomas Menino

admitted it was a mistake to broker an agreement that could have given South Boston, still perceived three decades after the busing crisis as a hostile white enclave, $65 million in benefits in exchange for cooperation on a new convention center.

As recently as August of 2003, the highest-ranking African American in state politics, Senator Dianne Wilkerson of Boston, said division remains the rule, not the exception. She has been the only African American in the state senate for the last decade.

"I'm tired of hearing people bragging about Boston as a changing city and that we have 50.5 percent people of color when in fact they're not reflected anywhere in the city's fabric," Wilkerson told the Associated Press. "The resistance to breaking the economic barriers have been incredibly hard. They are as much alive today in Massachusetts as they were fifty years ago in the most segregated part of the South. And I was born in Arkansas."

And that is where many African Americans leave it. It is why many professionals never come here in the first place. It is why many leave Boston upon their graduation from the numerous colleges in the area. It is why many come here for entry-level positions and then talk about bolting for supposedly blacker pastures before even paying their first month's rent. Common for me in the early 1990s was to go to parties and count on the conversation eventually turning toward trashing Boston's tokenism and social isolation. After a few of those evenings, some people seemed so desperate to get out of Dodge, I thought they were willing to go to Dodge City, Kansas.

To leave it like that would be a huge mistake. Boston is not yet a model for race relations, but many African Americans have established local and national models of progress, in the spirit of Frederick Douglass, who said in Boston in 1865, "No class of men can, without insulting their own nature, be content with any deprivation of their rights."

Community organizers from around the nation have for years hailed the Dudley Street Neighborhood Initiative (DSNI) as a model for how residents can bring back a forsaken part of a city. In the mid-1980s, DSNI pioneered the concept of ordinary citizens taking vacant land by eminent domain and building homes. The neighborhood is as bright a rainbow as there is in Boston, mostly African American, Latino, and Cape Verdean, but with some white residents, too.

Born in Boston, John Barros, the thirty-year-old executive director of DSNI in 2004, left the city to attend Dartmouth College and lived for a while in New York City. Barros told the *Globe* in 2001 that Boston "has a lot of potential, but it will only be realized if people are going to stay and help stabilize the community. Growing up as a family, we were always conscious that we needed to come back and try to make an impact."

The former executive director, Greg Watson, told me in 1998, "Right now, people just know us for getting the land. Ten years from now, we want people to know Dudley Street for what it did with the land."

\*   \*   \*

In the 1990s Boston was arguably the nation's top city in reducing youth violence. The city went without a juvenile murder for a twenty-nine-month span from mid-1995 to late 1997. African American ministers were on the streets and in the prisons. Wealthier black men and women, and health and recreation centers and churches, created afterschool and weekend mentoring groups. Police crackdowns helped, but just as important were African American judges who tried to look at each individual case to see if offenders could be rehabilitated instead of just being thrown in jails that breed frustration and future violence.

Keith Motley, in 2004 the vice chancellor for student affairs at the University of Massachusetts in Boston and in the forefront of community mentoring efforts, told me in 1997 about a former gang member who walked up to him on a subway to thank him. Motley said the man said to him, "You fed me, you never counted me out. Now I'm married, with a boy. I moved out of the environment."

The spirit of the antiviolence efforts can be summed up in the person of Tina Cherry. Her son, Louis Brown, was a youth worker shot on his way to a meeting. For several years, she has held an annual walk for peace in Dorchester. After the 2003 march, where she was a fireball of energy, jogging back and forth among walkers and leading chants, she told me: "What's coming out of me is rage. If I don't get it out this way, it comes out in a different way that is self-destructive. It's not like I'm happy today and sad tomorrow. It's not a back-and-forth thing. The energy I'm showing is really two things that are with me all the time. There is the anger of what happened, an anger that will never go away. Part of me is gone. But part of me is still here. We still live. We now have a lesson to teach. We have no control over what happened to our children. But we have choices. We are still alive. That's what I want people to see."

Some African Americans have succeeded in arenas that are the least seen or taken for granted. One example is Jet-A-Way, a waste-disposal and recycling company founded in the 1960s by African Americans Eddie and Darlene Jeter. Eddie died in 1991, but under Darlene's leadership, the firm was in the 2002 *Waste Age* 100, a listing of the nation's top private companies in the waste industry, with $16 million in revenues.

Back in 1990, Darlene told me that the business survived and thrived despite some unfair scrutiny from businesses. "One guy who hired us kept calling to tell us to be on time and collect the stuff right," she said. "After two years of [our] doing the job right, he called up and said he was sorry. He realized he was nervous about us because we were black."

Among the forces trying to help nervous young African American professionals stay in Boston is the Partnership. Run by Benaree Wiley, the Partnership is a nonprofit group that mentors newcomers in the hopes that they stay to move up into the management and executive ranks of area businesses. Wiley keeps the heat on businesses, with periodic publishing of statistics that suggest that some of Boston's stereotypes as a closed old-boy shop are still deserved. In 2003 African Americans made up only 4.4 percent of Boston's professional workers and only 3.1 percent of senior managers and executives. Suffolk County, which includes Boston, is 22 percent black.

Wiley, one of the most optimistic women in the city, has said, "I think we're beginning to build a critical mass of black professionals." But she also said, in a *Globe* guest column she cowrote with Paul Guzzi, president of the Greater Boston Chamber of Commerce, "If [black professionals] do not see an opportunity to advance, they will leave."

Of similar mind is the architect David Lee of Stull and Lee. The firm has designed many buildings around the nation, including, locally, the Boston Police Headquarters and, afar, the American Jazz Museum and the Negro Leagues Baseball Museum, both in Kansas City. On the one hand, Lee, like Wiley, minces no words about the fact that it remains tougher for black firms to attain the same level of prominence in Boston as white firms. Lee said in 2001, "It's about as tough for a minority firm to get a major commission in the private sector as it is for a minority to get a major head-coach position in Division I sports or the NFL. The reality is, if you look at most of the work minority firms get, it's disproportionately in the public sector.... It's very difficult to compete in a hard economy for glamorous projects when the core of your work is public projects."

But Lee has stayed because of driving optimism that he can "be stuck in traffic on my way to Logan Airport some night and look up at the Boston skyline and see the lights of a building I designed."

Untold other African Americans have stayed as well or have made Boston their base. In the academic arena, civil rights scholars such as Charles Ogletree, Lani Guinier, and Randall Kennedy are at Harvard. Deval Patrick, who President Clinton picked to replace Guinier after withdrawing her nomination to head the Civil Rights Division of the Department of Justice, came from the Boston area. Christopher Edley, who was one of Clinton's top advisers on race and in 2003 became the first African American dean of a top-ranked law school, at the University of California at Berkeley, had been at Harvard Law School. Activist reverend Charles Stith became Clinton's ambassador to Tanzania.

While Boston has yet to have a mayor of color, African Americans have held or hold the posts of district attorney and sheriff for Suffolk County. Chuck Turner has proven that one can go from community activist working for years among the city's poorest residents, residents who supposedly do not vote, to election to the Boston City Council.

Across the river, Cambridge in the 1990s had the nation's first openly gay African American mayor, Ken Reeves. African Americans have worked as hard in Boston as anywhere else to preserve history. Boston and Cambridge have African American Freedom Trails, and Beacon Hill has the restored African Meeting House—the oldest standing African American church in the United States—to go along with the more well-known Freedom Trail. The nation's longest running production of Langston Hughes's Black Nativity, founded by the late Elma Lewis, has become by far the most integrated cultural event in Boston. Nationally renowned painters Allan Rohan Crite and Paul Goodnight reside here. Some of the nation's most painful racial history was preserved in a small studio in Boston's South End, where the late Henry Hampton and his crew at Blackside produced the public-television epic *Eyes on the Prize*.

Other African Americans had their eyes on the prize of commercial television. From 1982 to 1986, Boston broke ground as the city with the highest level of black ownership of a major network affiliate, Channel 7. The spirit of the investors in trying to change the image of African Americans in white-run media was symbolized by the late Ruth Batson, who spent the 1960s and 1970s fighting for school desegregation. She said in 1982, "It's not going to be easy. It's going to be tough. I have a small amount of stock, but as director, I have one vote and a big mouth that I've never been reluctant to use."

There are many African Americans who continue to live out Batson's philosophy. The African American–founded Boston Bank of Commerce, serving neighborhoods often overlooked by the white-run banks, has been so successful that its operations have expanded to Miami and Los Angeles under the new name of One United Bank. It has become the first interstate African American–run bank in the nation.

One United CEO Kevin Cohee said in early 2003, "What this is about is trying to show that some of the dreams and aspirations that Martin Luther King and African American people have had over the years are starting to manifest themselves in concrete, tangible achievements. Our institution is truly an outgrowth of what happened in the civil rights era. It's sort of like the dream coming true."

One key African American woman who is trying to make sure that the big banks, at least her big bank, Bank of America, does not overlook historically underserved communities is Gail Snowden.

The daughter of 1960s and 1970s civil rights and education pioneers Otto and Muriel Snowden, Gail is in charge of Bank of America's strategic national relationships and has been a leader in community development banking here and across the country.

While African Americans still have a tough time cracking the top ranks of power in the business world, there has been more progress in the nonprofit sector. The United Way of Massachusetts Bay has been one of the most successful nonprofits in the nation. Under Marian Heard, the first African American to run a major United Way chapter, a half billion dollars was raised between 1992 and 2003. If there is a symbol of optimism in Boston, she is it. Part of the reason is that she is also a symbol of what can happen when people of color feel welcome in Boston, to the point of her saying that she has not personally experienced discrimination in the city.

"No matter what the surveys say, this is a generous town," Heard told the *Globe* in 2003. "Boston, the United Way, the *Globe,* and the *Herald* all made an effort in welcoming me. The United Way printed and mailed thousands of flyers with my picture so people knew I was not only the first woman, but also the first woman of color in a major United Way city. People reached out so much that after about fifty receptions and dinners, I had to say, 'Please, happy to come, happy to speak, and I want to meet you, but please, no food.'...I get cabs late at night. In fact, people at garages walk me to my car. Now, I do extend myself. I go back to them and take a small bag of candy."

Rev. Ray Hammond, who became known as one of the ministers fighting youth violence, chairs the Boston Foundation, which distributes $50 million a year in grants, focusing heavily on youth programs. Hammond, an African American man, follows in the legacy of former foundation president Anna Faith Jones, an African American woman who ran the foundation for fifteen years until 2001.

Jones was the first African American woman in the nation to run a community foundation. Under her, the endowment soared from $100 million to more than $700 million. Hammond said of Jones, "She never saw poor or disadvantaged communities as being without assets, and she always worked to develop those assets."

You can find black folks in Boston in the oddest places, odd if you do not expect to find them there. A friend of mine, Talmadge Mentall, was president of the Amateur Telescope Makers of Boston, is an editorial assistant at *Sky and Telescope,* and has a comet named after him. The Boston Red Sox, long disparaged for its history of shunning black players, had in the 1990s a black female public-address announcer and gave baseball its first African American female assistant general manager. While Louis Farrakhan of the Nation of Islam is considered a pariah outside of the black community, the leader of the Nation of Islam's Boston mosque, Don Muhammad, has long had an open pipeline to City Hall. While the national Boy Scouts of America have stood by the expulsion of gay leaders elsewhere in the nation, an African American downtown lawyer, Richard Soden, has helped the Boston Minuteman Council become the nation's first Scout council to include sexual orientation in its nondiscrimination policy.

There is no getting around the fact that the Boston Public Schools leave as much to be desired as urban public schools around the nation. The Boston system arguably has the most dramatic two-tier cleavage in the nation. Boston Latin, now a de facto disproportionately white preserve, has a $19 million endowment, the largest in the nation for a public school. Despite the budget cuts for the rest of the system, its alumni raised another $35 million in 2003. "You are not going to change the Boston public school system unless you are prepared to go for broke," said Hubie Jones, founder of the approximately thirty-member school board. "This is a wake-up call."

But for the optimist, there are many individual victories that hold out the tantalizing hope that if there ever came a time that the nation truly valued its youth, Boston could be a national leader in doing public education right. Pilot schools in Boston such as Fenway High, the Boston Arts Academy, and the Media and Technology Charter School prove that if you keep schools to a humane size and create high expectations, young people can dream of college and become critical thinkers. I went to a Boston Arts Academy play in 2003 where I was thrilled to see youths attack portrayals of their image as thuggish, "booty-shaking" rappers on Black Entertainment Television. Boston is a cauldron of nationally influential education thinking, from Harvard's Civil Rights Project, which has warned mightily of the resegregation of schools, to the nationally used Algebra Project of civil rights warrior Bob Moses, to Jeffrey Howard's Efficacy Institute, which consults with school systems around the nation about the importance of high expectations. Boston is also a nationally watched laboratory in the controversial world of charter schools, supported by groups such as the Pioneer Institute.

* * *

I do not know what happened to that young man who told me at Roxbury Community College that "black folks can't get anywhere in this town." But I have seen youths who decided to go somewhere in Boston. My favorite story is from the early 1990s, when I mentored the student newspaper class at Jeremiah E. Burke High School.

Burke High School was then at ground zero in terms of youth violence. I told the class that I would be their mentor if they did me one favor. I wanted them to go to the Out of Town news kiosk in Harvard Square and get a non–East Coast newspaper. I hoped that a newspaper from somewhere else in the country could show them that there was a whole world outside their neighborhoods. This task did not seem like heavy lifting, since the students talked often of going to concerts forty-five minutes away in Providence and Worcester.

But three months later, only half the class had made it to Out of Town. I asked them why they couldn't keep their end of the bargain, since all it took was a subway ride.

One student said, "Because we feel we don't belong there." That sent me off into an Old Black Fart speech about how people died for your right to walk freely in this country. Eventually, everyone went to Out of Town. The newspaper the kids worked on became more hard-hitting. About eight years later, in 1998, one of those students turned up as an assistant real estate assessor for the City of Boston.

The fellow, Sam DePina, had once been shot in the leg by youths, but recovered to become class president, join the school newspaper, break up fights in the halls, and graduate from the Burke in 1992. He then attended the University of Massachusetts at Boston. I ended up writing a column about how he gave a plaque of thanks in 1997 to his high school headmaster, Al Holland. DePina said that Holland "made me feel like I could take the initiative in things that were positive. I had never remotely done anything like run for class president. But he [Holland] said, 'We need people like you to take charge.'"

Just as meaningful to Holland as the plaque was something else that DePina did for him. The two went to lunch. "We went down to this deli that serves the best sandwiches in town," Holland said. "When I started to pay, he pulled my arm back and said, 'You've done enough for me. It's my turn to treat you.'"

That is the hope behind the headlines. DePina, who as a youth had faced death's door, was working for the city, getting somewhere, for himself and the city of Boston. Whatever problems there remain in this town, he will be one of its solutions. Quiet as this hope is kept, it is why many people of color come to Boston and actually stay. We never give up thinking that this city can be a solution that helps the rest of the nation cure its ills.

# A Literary Landscape:
# From Jamaica to Boston

*Patricia Powell*

I used to think that I became a writer by accident, that a career in economics was where I was headed until I began failing advanced economics and had to switch to English literature. But I have since come to believe that there are no accidents. That all along I was meant to be a writer. And that my early childhood experiences—of separation from my mother, of being raised by my great-aunt, who was perpetually on the brink of death, of the mystery surrounding my birth father, and of being united with my mother years later in a foreign country—were not accidents of birth, but were experiences meant to mark me so profoundly that they would become the grist that I would spend the next twenty years of my life milling. And I feel too that it is no accident that the place where all of this would happen was Boston—the city where I have met, one by one, all the people who would propel me in the direction of a literary life, the city where I would develop all the tools necessary to live out a writer's life.

We arrived at Logan Airport in the heart of winter, my brother and sister and I. My mother, who had fled years earlier to Boston from Jamaica to escape her marriage, and had settled here, met us at the airport. In batches of twos and threes, she had sent for her children, and my siblings and I were the last batch. She bundled us up immediately into thick warm coats, for against that fierce New England cold our flimsy clothes were like pieces of tissue paper, and hurried us to the car waiting at the curb that would take us to the section of Boston called Dorchester. I was sixteen, and I had never before been outside Jamaica. I had never seen real snow, and from the back of the slow-moving car, it did not have the clean white powdery look I often saw on the postcards my uncle sent from Canada with money. This snow had been piled up on the sides of the road for days, and was blackened with dirt and the exhaust from the many cars and trucks that hurtled by; pieces of garbage clung to the snow, and dogs, it seemed, had found neat little places to defecate.

From the front of the car, my mother bombarded us with a steady stream of questions about all the relatives and friends she had left in Jamaica. Just a few years behind me in age, Dermot and Jacqueline were happy to see her again, and they filled her in on all the details. But I didn't have answers for any of my mother's questions and even if I did, my answers were short and blunt. I was not happy to see my mother, for my mother and I were not friends. I did not understand why, of all her children, I was the one she had sent away at three months and had never reclaimed until now. And I wanted to know the details of the mystery surrounding my birth father. I didn't know these people. I had never been very friendly with any of my immediate family members, except for an older brother, and yet here I was thrust suddenly into this newly assembled, makeshift family, after sixteen years of estrangement, and in this cold, strange place. I was furious and I was desperately missing my great-aunt Nora, the woman who raised me and who was really my mother. And I was terrified. But this wintry city was to be my home and the place where another phase of my life was beginning, and I felt that my only choice was to settle down into this new existence, in this unknown city that was said by everyone to be a place full of opportunities.

Our yellow house in Dorchester was located on a residential street lined with close-together houses: a jumble of triple-deckers, Queen Annes, mansard-roofed duplexes, stone and brick apartment rows, and even a few Victorians that had known grander days and were crumbling now. There was not a patch of green to be seen anywhere, just the collar of dirt at the mouth of each yard and some scraggly looking trees, naked without leaves. Kids desperate for a place to shoot hoops and to hang out after school turned an empty lot on the adjacent street into their playground. From our living room windows, we could hear them hooting and shrieking and we envied them. For unless there was a special request to go to the store or to the post office, we were forbidden to leave the house. My mother foresaw all the many evils that she imagined might promptly befall us on the city's streets, and she threatened all manner of punishments should we disobey her. What else was there to do but to turn inward —to read, to squabble over board games, to watch reruns on television, and to long for my great-aunt's house in Grove Place, the garden full of yellow bells and ostrich plumes, and to dream of the willow trees at the bottom of the veranda where I dozed on so many Sunday afternoons after the big meal.

Our part of Dorchester near Grove Hall, and on the border of Roxbury, was a predominantly working-class and black neighborhood. The Jews and Irish who once lived in this section of town had long since escaped to the suburbs, and before them, the wealthy Bostonians who had made this area their safe quiet getaway when Dorchester was still a country landscape, a retreat from the city proper. Familiar as they may have looked to me, the American black people of Dorchester were definitely not the same stock as the black people I had grown up around in Jamaica. They did not sing out their greetings the way we did, their accents had their own strange clipped ring. When they walked they did not roll their hips in the same fashion, and the spices that we used to season our meats, our thick, rich, hot pepper sauces, were not easy to find here, and when my mother did find them, she complained that they were expensive. Still, they were my people, and if I looked deeply into their faces when they flung their heads back for the laughter to peal out, I could see traces of some of my cousins I had left behind, and that was comforting. The tiny commercial strip not far from my house boasted a barbershop, a hairdressing salon where my mother went to get her perm, a liquor store, a used-furniture store, a ribs-and-chicken joint that always had a good smell wafting from it, a grocery-variety shop that sold everything imaginable, even wigs, and a house of beauty. My mother warned us never to linger in that area. But every evening after school, I made that strip part of my route home, for the sidewalk was always crowded with people laughing and talking and the streets were always thick with traffic and with loud music blaring from car speakers, and now and again a door would jingle open as I was passing, and I would catch a glimpse of a head frying under an enormous dryer or a man grinning with a woman and looking at her with eyes that said everything.

That first winter living in Boston, there never seemed to be enough light. Night came promptly at four-thirty and I was rarely ever truly warm, no matter what I wore. I thought constantly of Jamaica's long, hot, dusty days, of the everlasting heat and those rainstorms that could bear down heavily on us for five steady minutes, but in the end, roads would disappear, houses would flood, and animals would be washed away. And I thought constantly, too, of my great-aunt Nora whom I missed terribly and of the shop she owned, which was the hub of the entire community and the place where I spent much of my childhood. As I remember it, the shop was open all day and all night and was flooded with men who came to drink and to smoke and to talk about politics and to burst open their wounds. Sometimes men would quarrel and threaten each other with cutlasses, and fights would break out, and my great-aunt like a large bird would swoop down in their midst and try to soothe the steaming tempers. The annual street dance where winning couples received cash prizes was held right outside the shop's piazza, and during elections the politicians drove up in vans and broadcast from their loudspeakers promises they would never deliver. Strangers from abroad wandering the countryside often stopped in for a drink at my great-aunt's shop and dazzled us with their tales of travel. On Easter, and again at Christmas and New Year's, the two merry-go-rounds in the field across the road would turn, and vendors would set up stalls and sell food and homemade ice cream flavored with rum and rose water, and the musicians would strike up a tune, and the ravenous dogs would be joyful again for there was so much to eat. And I, too, would be happy for there would be no end to the bands of children available for play.

But that world was gone, and here in front of me like a rude awakening was Boston, my new home. A few blocks from my house was Muhammad Mosque Number Eleven, where Malcolm X used to worship, and around the corner from the mosque was the Jeremiah E. Burke High School. My mother immediately enrolled us at the Burke, where I would meet three women who were to set me firmly on a course to become a writer. As if my great-aunt had sent word telling her that I was coming and that she should take good care of me, Miss Spencer, my English and homeroom teacher, adopted me at once. Like my great-aunt she was larger than life and friendly and talkative and good. Like my great-aunt she had a rich and complicated laugh, knew all the right people, and wielded, or so it seemed to me at least, a great deal of power. I loved her at once, and she too adored me. Almost as if she had been waiting for me to leave so that she, too, could leave, my great-aunt died the following spring. And afterward, my relationship with my mother just turned ugly and bitter. But it helped matters that I was bright and could easily sink myself vigorously into work. Miss Spencer became a great friend and mentor. In 1984, when I graduated from the Burke as the class valedictorian and was heading off to Wellesley College to study economics, she handed me an anthology of black women writers in which she inscribed this message: *I hope one day to see your name among all these writers.* To this day, it is still not clear to me what she saw, for I did not write stories in her class, and becoming a writer was the last thing on my mind. At that time, I wanted to be a businesswoman like my great-aunt had been; I wanted to follow in her shoes.

Situated just at the edge of Dorchester on the Columbia Point peninsula, which it shares with the John F. Kennedy Presidential Library, is UMass, Boston's preeminent urban institution of higher education. Founded in 1964 to provide superior education at moderate cost, and to address the needs of its students who come from varied social, cultural, and ethnic backgrounds, UMass regularly initiates educational and social programs meant to effect change in its neighboring urban community. Urban Scholars is one such program—designed to allow high school students from impoverished schools to take college-level courses that will increase their chances of getting into and staying in first-rate colleges. In 1982, three high schools were chosen for the pilot program, among them the Burke, and of course, Miss Spencer signed me up at once. Through the Urban Scholars Program, I met the poet Kate Rushin, and Joan Becker, the director. Like Miss Spencer before them, these two women took me under their wings at once.

It is hard to say what it might have been about me in those days that pulled such good people to me, people who only wanted to help me. Though I had no particular religious leanings at the time, I attributed all this good fortune to the spirit of my great-aunt. I was deeply convinced that every good soul I encountered was a person she had gotten in touch with ahead of time and told to help pave my way. In my mind my great-aunt was more powerful dead than alive and, like the angels, could move around more freely and run interference on my behalf. To this day, I still believe that this is how I managed, for back then I felt as if something inside me, some door, had immediately shrieked shut the moment I landed in Boston. And for years, I lived feeling like a boat being tossed about on the turbulent sea of life, completely without direction but open nonetheless to the shifts of the wind. Only later would I come to learn that this roiling sea of life stretched out before me was nothing to shy away from, nothing to cower before, but something to run toward fiercely.

I grew up in a post-independence Jamaica, which meant that by the time I went to school in the 1970s, Britain had loosened her grip on our educational system somewhat. Alongside Shakespeare and Milton and Hardy, I remember reading V. S. Naipaul, Sam Selvon, and Andrew Salkey. And at home there were all the radio plays narrated in dialect that I religiously followed every night. As my great-aunt was often busy at the shop and at the many board meetings she chaired, reading became a great friend. In addition to the allotment I was allowed to borrow on each visit, I regularly stole books from the public library, stuffing them underneath my school uniform and scowling my way past the librarian at the desk. In the Urban Scholars Program that first summer, Kate Rushin fed us a rich diet of African American poetry and prose, and in that course, I was introduced for the first time to Paule Marshall's *Brown Girl, Brownstones,* a coming-of-age novel about a girl growing up in Brooklyn with homesick Barbadian parents. I read the novel over and over, for I knew these people keenly. I could identify with all the characters for I had lived out all their experiences. I knew the mother who was forever working and saving to make ends meet, and the husband who had turned into a complete stranger to her. I recognized the foods they ate and the yearnings they carried in their chests for that place back home, for the tastes of things on their tongues and the feel of the skin in a particular kind of heat that could soak your clothes in minutes. My papers and journal entries on the novel must have been extremely passionate, for Kate was aghast when I told her I wanted to study accounting to become a CPA, a certified public accountant. One afternoon, Joan, who was a Wellesley alumna, pulled me out of class and drove me to the college campus to show me around and to implore me to apply and major in English if I got in. It was my junior year by then; I was busily preparing for the SATs and applying to colleges that offered a business major. I had only been living in the United States a year. I knew nothing about the Ivy League schools or about the famous Seven Sisters. I knew nothing about social capital and how it worked in this country. But these women knew everything, and they steered me toward one of America's finest schools.

Maybe one can never really be ready for the social and cultural world of such an elite institution as Wellesley. But in some strange way, I felt ready. Growing up in Jamaica, a predominantly black society, I was well aware of the perniciousness of class, though not of race, even as I understood colorism very well, prejudice based on skin shade. And without my knowing it, in its own peculiar way that little community in Dorchester had been slowly grooming me, preparing me for the transition to the world outside its border, helping me to make a more manageable leap from Manchester, Jamaica, to Wellesley, Massachusetts, one of the nation's wealthiest suburbs. Like many other predominantly white, elite institutions, Wellesley had its fair share of racial incidents which were frequently reported in the college newspaper. But as far as I knew and was able to allow myself to acknowledge, I did not experience racism per se, partly because I didn't really know it, couldn't readily recognize it in its subtler shades, and probably because I refused to see it, so thick was the protective gauze I had wound around myself. At Wellesley, I enrolled in women's studies and black studies classes. I took American history courses and a class on South Africa's apartheid regime. Weekly, I watched as police carted away loads of women as they held anti-apartheid marches and disrupted classes with their demonstrations against Wellesley's investments in South Africa. Slowly I began to wake up to the full meanings of what oppression was. Slowly I began to acquire a social and political consciousness. Wellesley, Massachusetts, was a far cry from Dorchester, but both of these metropolitan Boston communities were opening up my eyes to the complexity and unevenness of life in America and the world beyond and leaving indelible marks.

When I began writing stories for the first time, in an introductory fiction class taught by Robert Polito at Wellesley, it was a way of bringing my great-aunt back to life: her deep laughter that rang into the hills, her beautiful teeth with the sliver of gold in the middle, her dimpled cheeks, her voice when she was quarreling with me over something valuable I had broken. The cancer that eventually killed her was the same cancer she had been suffering from for as long as I knew her. In that class, as I was writing the first chapter of what would become my first novel, I remembered how Aunt Nora was always sipping from a flask of brandy because there was always some pain somewhere in her body, there was always some ache, always some bad feeling, that only a little sip would quell. Many afternoons I would lie in bed with her, playing cards or just watching her doze off. Sometimes I would lie with my head against her belly and the steady beat of her heart would put me to sleep. Other times, I stayed awake and daydreamed and talked to myself and sang. And even now, I still write in bed, in longhand with a pencil on sheets of white paper, and I think all of that has to do with all those years growing up and spending time with her in bed and getting comfort from the smell of the essences she dabbed behind her ears or the castor oil she rubbed in her hair, or the feel of my head on her belly, and the steady beating heart.

My head was obviously not cut out for business, for I swiftly began failing my economics classes. But as it also turned out, my head was not cut out for a great many things, for while I may have been an excellent student at the Burke, at Wellesley I was barely average. That first creative writing class was at the suggestion of a friend who saw me suffering over the physics requirement and took pity. The first two stories I wrote were in standard English, one about a Haitian doctor turned Boston taxi driver who is going home for the first time in twenty years, the other about a relationship between a girl and her older male lover. But my final story, which was written in Jamaican English and which eventually became the opening chapter of my book *Me Dying Trial,* received much favorable feedback from my teacher and classmates. I was a quiet and shy student, hardly said two words, but I was an attentive listener and I was receptive to their comments, their evaluation of the characters. I received a good grade in the writing course, and the following semester I enrolled in another one, this time with the novelist Jonathan Strong, who would end up becoming my thesis adviser and dear friend. I turned in the Haitian story, which I had reworked, and the dialect story. Again, the dialect story was clearly a favorite and the students talked about the richness of the characters, the story's vivid descriptions, its emotional impact. That feedback spurred me on. I wrote page after page, feverishly, unable to stop. And my classmates looked forward to each new installment even though it was a difficult read, for the dialect was not easy. But I wanted to preserve this authentic Jamaican speech, giving voice to those people in the shop who had had little to no schooling and whose only means of communication were through this rich, colorful vernacular.

After graduation from Wellesley, I took an office job in Newton, an apartment in Somerville, and I sat down to revise the novel. At Café Pamplona in Harvard Square, at Panini in Somerville, and at 1369 in Inman Square, in cafés all over the city, I wrote for hours buried under sheaves of papers and nursing that sole cup of coffee. At

Wellesley, I had mostly been secluded on campus, hardly ever venturing into the city to attend readings by visiting speakers; now I combed the papers daily, searching for venues to nourish my writing. And there were places galore, so many bookstores, colleges, libraries, not to mention the innumerable coffee shops, bars, church basements, and living rooms where writers convened to read and share work. Boston has a famous and thriving literary community, bubbling with energy, and yet for a long time I stayed on its edges, curious yet uncertain of my own footing, my place in it. Even as excerpts of my manuscript were being published, even as PEN New England, Boston's preeminent literary organization, awarded me the PEN New England Discovery prize, I felt that my stories, my great tome of a novel, were different from the work of other writers in this city, so strange and exotic compared to everyone else's words, and I was self-conscious.

In the spring of 1989, my Jamaican friend Ian died of AIDS. He died in New York, and although his family operated a church in Brooklyn and his mother was a minister, Ian died alone. His family had rejected him when they found out he was sick and that he was gay. In my mind, it was this rejection, this disappointment that ultimately killed Ian. Two things happened in Providence, Rhode Island, where I moved a few months after Ian's death to attend graduate school: I started to write about Boston, a place where I had been living for eight years; and I started to write about AIDS, the gay community, and homophobia. In 1982, when I left Jamaica, there had been no mention of AIDS, though there was definitely a thriving gay community centered in Kingston, which was also the hub of gay life: the cruising areas, the clubs, the support groups, the drag balls that attracted hundreds, the gay newspaper. Only a couple of years later in the United States, however, AIDS would already be everywhere—on television, in the papers, on the radio, around me, on the streets, in the supermarkets, at the night clubs and bars I frequented. Everywhere one turned, staring you in the eye was the awful specter of AIDS.

The novel that emerged from this time of writing, *A Small Gathering of Bones*, is dedicated to Ian, and it is about a group of gay men living in Jamaica during the 1970s and dealing with a mysterious disease. I chose the Jamaican dialect for this story so that the experiences would feel authentic. After all, it is the language of Jamaica, the language of its people, and these gay men are Jamaica's children even though they are regularly stoned to death, murdered, their mutilated bodies washed up on shores or found broken in bushes. But though the language of the book is Jamaica, and the setting too is Jamaica, the heart of the novel is inexorably Boston. As I wrote, I thought vividly of not only Jamaica's vibrant gay community, but of Boston's own socially and politically active gay community. I wrote thinking of the autonomous spaces here in Boston that gay men and lesbians have created in order to meet and socialize freely, to network with each other, to provide therapeutic counseling, and to create a sense of solidarity and community without fear of reprisals. And I thought, too, of the care systems that had to be quickly generated as we dealt with the devastating impact of AIDS, and of the deep friendships that often took the place of familial bonds, as so many gay men and lesbians are estranged from their families.

In 1991, when I was twenty-five years old and fresh out of graduate school with two manuscripts under contract to the English publisher Heinemann, I returned to Boston to begin my teaching career at the University of Massachusetts. My students there ranged in age from eighteen to eighty-one, and though the task of teaching them seemed completely daunting at first, I had no choice but to simply share with them everything I had learned from all my teachers before, to invite them to read all the books I had read, and to attend to their stories with the same kind of care and enthusiasm that had been given mine. By the end of my first semester, I also began to share with them all the little pieces of information about writing that I was beginning to garner for myself. At UMass, I was on my own for the first time. I had neither mentors nor a bevy of graduate students and advisers to help me. To find support and community, I became involved in a writers group, and even joined the Writers Union briefly. Still I was lonely. I was coming into myself now and was beginning to wonder about home again but in an entirely different way.

One day at the Somerville café Panini, where I had gone to grade papers, a young woman showed up in my mind's eyes. She was about sixteen or seventeen and her race then was indeterminable to me, though she was decidedly Jamaican. But as she emerged further and wanted to know the origins of her father who was part Chinese, part black, I found her desires curious, as my own father had been an enigma to me. I packed up my papers and straightaway hurried home to look up Chinese immigration in my history books, but there was nothing to be found except a paragraph on indentureship. That desire to know this character's father's Asian origins led me back to Jamaica (for only the second time in over a decade) to research the history of the Chinese who have lived there since the nineteenth century but whose contributions to Jamaican culture and society have often been minimized.

What were the circumstances that drove these people away from China and brought them to the faraway Caribbean to live? What were their experiences like, leaving their country and their families so far away and coming over as laborers stacked up inside those ships? And if they survived the turbulent crossing, what were the working conditions like on those sugar plantations, where just a few years earlier African slavery was in full bloom? My third novel, *The Pagoda,* is a story about Chinese immigration to Jamaica. Set during the nineteenth century, it follows the experiences of Lowe, a Chinese woman passing as a male shopkeeper. What did it feel like for Lowe to inhabit a body that now had to speak a new language and live in a landscape so utterly unfamiliar and to be caught up in the middle of the country's racial and political preoccupations? How did Lowe and the other Chinese immigrants decide who could be trusted, who could be a friend, so that they could create community? How did they manage in this foreign territory as they reinvented themselves in order to fit, sometimes doing it literally, as in the case of Lowe, my main character, who cross-dresses and passes as a male to survive, to establish a sense of belonging?

To write *The Pagoda,* I drew deeply on my experiences as a person of color, a foreigner who had immigrated to North America and who after many years was still not quite at home here. In this novel, I could ask questions that all immigrants must ask. Where do I fit, and who am I, really? What does it mean to have a foot in each world and not belong to either one? What does it mean to belong and how does one go about finding a community, carving out a niche? Where exactly is home, and what constitutes one? Is home a place, or a feeling inside the chest that you carry around with you? In Jamaica I had never been an "other." I was the status quo. And I was at home in that world. But in my new city of Boston, everything was different from what I was used to, the language and climate and landscape and people, the politics of race and gender and sexuality, the challenges of being an other. The self that had grown up in Jamaica could not survive here in the same way; a new self had to be imagined. Internal resources I didn't know I possessed had to be called up. By the end of *The Pagoda*, Lowe no longer wants to live a split existence, with one foot in one world, the other foot in another. She wants integration, wholeness; she wants solidity. By the end of my writing the novel I, too, wanted those things.

As 2004 began, I was at work on a new novel, which I think may be my last Jamaican novel. Twenty-two years have passed since my arrival at Logan Airport. My accent has begun to fade and Jamaica too is starting to fade, the pictures of the faces and the terrain, the sound of the voices, of their song. Now when I return to Jamaica, it is no longer laden with strong memories; it is no longer a place charged with longing; it has become a part of me. This new novel is about a man who returns to Jamaica to bury his father after a twenty-five-year estrangement. He has a full life here in Boston, with all the physical trappings of home, a house in the country surrounded by trees full of birds, a teaching job at a nearby university, a steady relationship. But he is going back to bury his father, whom he hasn't spoken to in all these years, and to bury a very troubled past, to close that chapter finally, so he can free himself to fully pursue the rest of his life. The experiences there will be his trial through fire, and he will come out on the other side a little softer and with more of a core. Perhaps this time when he returns home to Boston, he'll finally be able to see the city in which he lives in the way that it really is and with its own particular characteristics. He will come to learn that to really embrace a place, you have to thoroughly and completely let go of the other one.

In 2003 I was offered a job in California. I was ready to go, my books were packed up in boxes, I was already dreaming of the heat and the sun; the realtor had begun showing my place here in Boston. And then, at the last minute, I decided to stay. Just like that. I had no job lined up here. I had no love waiting. But I decided to stay, to make Boston my home. It was a leap and it required faith. But I accepted the challenge. I wanted to see if indeed I could grow wings. The year after making that decision felt like my very first year in Boston. I felt as if I was living here in this city with brand-new eyes. I moved fifteen minutes away into what feels like the country though it is only a metropolitan suburb, but there are trees around me now, and I have learned their names and the names of birds. I lived through a bitter winter, and it was as if I was seeing snow for the first time. The spring was long and wet and chilly, and summer didn't come until mid-July. Every day I watched blue jays and robins and squirrels from my kitchen windows, busy at the feeder, and one by one, I saw the birch and the cherry trees clothe themselves in leaves, and I heard the boy next door striking the piano, and the neighbor's fat brown cat watched me steadily.

My mother, who now lives in Florida, recently came to visit. We took the train into downtown Boston and walked all over this famously walkable city. She wanted to see Haymarket again, the old Italian market near City Hall, where she and I used to go early on Saturday mornings to buy produce and fresh fish and goat meat and live crab for curried stew. At Faneuil Hall we stopped to have lunch, and then we wandered through the Public Gardens. We sat on a bench and admired the tall trees, the towering buildings, the thickets of flowers, and the kids on skateboards.

It is the first time that my mother has visited me since I left her yellow house in Dorchester at eighteen. It has taken us almost twenty years to get close. Patricia, she says to me, you alone here, you alone here in this cold place. You're not lonely? She pulls her sweater tighter around her, it's late June and we are still bundled up. It's my home, I say, smiling, a little alarmed at myself, for I've never said that before, that a place is my home, that Boston is my home. Not just this place where I live and work or go to school, but a place that I have chosen, a commitment that I have made to be fully present here, to be fully conscious. And in that moment I knew that for the first time, I was willing to let Jamaica recede into the background and allow Boston to emerge fully into the foreground. That I was ready now to face the city and its peculiarities. I was ready finally to be here, now.

# Innovation City

*Scott Kirsner*

I happened across the advertisement in a book about the invention of the telephone, and it transported me back to nineteenth-century Boston like a tumble down the rabbit hole. The shop being advertised, owned by one Charles Williams Jr., had opened in 1856, and it was the Circuit City of its day—if Circuit City made a practice of renting out its upstairs space to unproven inventors. The ad described Williams's business as a "Manufacturer of Telegraphic and Magnetical Apparatus, Galvanic Batteries, &c.," and as a wholesale and retail dealer in telegraph supplies. To the left of the ad copy was an etching of a cylindrical contraption that looked to me like a galvanic battery.

Charles Williams's shop, it turns out, is central to the history of technology in Boston, and I was curious to know whether it was still standing. I had seen a picture of the building, a stately, mansard-roofed structure, and I could easily imagine a Starbucks coffee shop now shoehorned into the first floor. A mapping Web site showed me that the address, 109 Court Street, would make Williams's shop a close neighbor of Faneuil Hall and the Old State House. I made several circuits of the meandering streets of downtown Boston before discovering that the old five-story building was long gone, supplanted by a government office tower and the edge of an empty brick plaza.

If I had been walking these streets in the latter half of the 1800s, in the years when Starbuck was still only a character in *Moby Dick*, 109 Court Street would have been the place to go to get a glimpse of the technological vanguard. The building was a hive of innovation—a patch of the future torn out and stitched roughly into the present. Downstairs, you could purchase your galvanic batteries; upstairs, Williams sublet space to a handful of obsessive tinkerers who were working on improvements to the telegraph, and on other projects as well.

Thomas Edison worked at 109 Court Street on the problem of sending more than one message down a telegraph wire simultaneously. (Edison perfected his first patented inventions—a vote-recording machine and a stock ticker—in Boston before leaving town, the result of a falling-out with his investors.) On the top floor of the building, a Scotsman named Alexander Graham Bell was whittling away at the same riddle that consumed Edison: how to wring more capacity out of a single telegraph wire. Bell had hired a worker from the shop downstairs, Thomas Watson, to help him with his experiments.

The duo eventually departed from their telegraph work, to the dismay of Bell's financial backers, who were certain that the biggest returns lay there. Instead, Bell and Watson built the first prototype telephone at 109 Court Street. The first residential phone line ran from 109 to Charles Williams's home in the city of Somerville, three miles northeast of Boston. In the years prior to 1879, every piece of telephone equipment sold in the world was manufactured at 109 Court; after that time, demand for the new technology was so great that Bell had to find other manufacturers to handle the overflow.

In 1916 a plaque was affixed to the exterior of 109 Court Street —"Here the Telephone Was Born"—and Alexander Graham Bell himself, now white-bearded, was present for the occasion. Today, although the building is gone, what happened inside it—the sort of nose-to-the-grindstone experimentation that sometimes yields breakthroughs that change the way we live, and other times just results in ground-down noses—continues in hundreds of other places around the metropolis.

No other city in America has been such a wellspring of innovation for so long. (And no other city has fretted so about losing its competitive advantage to other parts of the country, most recently to California's Silicon Valley.) For more than three hundred years, people have come to Boston to learn what has been done in their field thus far, stake a claim to an acre of the as-yet-undone, and begin tilling the hard soil.

Those innovators have produced a succession of new ideas that have enhanced and extended and forever altered our lives. The engineer who helped Bell draw up the patent for the telephone, an African American named Lewis Latimer, later made improvements to the filament of Edison's light bulb that extended its useful life from minutes to hours. Latimer also devised the threaded light bulb socket, paving the way for the development of the light bulb joke.

The guidance system that helped *Apollo 11* find its way from Cape Canaveral to the Sea of Tranquility was built in Boston. The venture capital industry and the first mutual fund have their roots here, as does the Ponzi scheme. General anesthesia was used for the first time in 1846 at Massachusetts General Hospital, and in Boston's Public Garden there is a monument to the miracle of being rendered unconscious before you are cut open. The iron lung was developed here, as was the pacemaker.

During World War II, scientists at MIT and Massachusetts-based Raytheon Company designed nearly half of all the radar equipment deployed during the war, devices that gave the Allies a critical edge. After the war, a Raytheon engineer realized that his microwave-emitting radar tubes were melting the chocolate bars he kept stashed in his back pocket, an insight that led to the microwave oven.

In 1944 Polaroid founder Edwin Land was on vacation in New Mexico when his three-year-old daughter asked why she couldn't look, right now, at the photograph he had just taken of her. Why indeed, Land wondered, and four years later the Polaroid Land Camera was available for purchase. In the late 1960s, a Cambridge firm called Bolt, Beranek and Newman won a contract from the government to build the first four nodes of the ARPANET, a computer network that eventually spawned the Internet. The first e-mail message in the world was sent by a researcher at the firm in 1971. Walter Gilbert, a Harvard-based researcher, helped launch the biotech revolution in the mid-1970s when he pioneered a method for rapidly reading the nucleotide sequences of DNA and RNA, work for which he later received the Nobel Prize. Gilbert was a founder of Biogen, one of the first wave of biotech start-ups, and he later became a chief proponent of the Human Genome Project. In 1979 the entrepreneur Dan Bricklin and the programmer Bob Frankston created the piece of software that helped propel personal computers into the workplace, the spreadsheet program VisiCalc. In one of the classrooms at Harvard Business School where Bricklin earned his MBA, there is a plaque that reads, "In this room in 1978, Dan Bricklin conceived of the first spreadsheet program." It refers to VisiCalc as "the original 'killer app' of the information age."

That building, Aldrich Hall, has not been demolished as of this writing.

\* \* \*

I knew there were other spots around Boston that I could visit to get a sense of the air of dogged inquisitiveness that must have permeated 109 Court Street. So I went looking for them. It happened to be Halloween the day I went to see a small company called iRobot, whose headquarters are located in an office park just off the Route 128 beltway that rings the city of Boston and its inner suburbs. Route 128 carries the boosterish label of "America's Technology Highway," and the suburbs that it connects have long been home to fast-growing tech companies.

The company's two founders were both dressed up in costume, as were most of the employees. Colin Angle, the boyish-looking chief executive, was dressed as a Deadhead, in shredded jeans and a tie-dyed T-shirt, headphones hanging around his neck. Helen Greiner, the company's president, seemed to have forgotten that it was a day for dressing up and had hastily put on an old blue lab coat and a few strings of Mardi Gras beads. Greiner and Angle first met as graduate students, working in robotics at MIT's Artificial Intelligence Lab, and upon receiving their degrees in 1990, launched the company together, along with one of their MIT professors, Rodney Brooks.

iRobot is an example of one kind of start-up company that thrives in the Boston area: an enterprise run by people consumed with the desire to introduce a new technology to the world—and no clear idea who will want it or why. Those who figure out the "who" and "why" before their money runs out survive.

At first, the company was based in Angle's living room, but its very first contract took the team far beyond living room scale: For NASA, Greiner, Angle and Brooks built a six-legged, insect-like robot named Attila, which was capable of clambering over rough terrain. NASA was trying to decide whether robots for Mars exploration should have wheels or legs. (Wheels, the agency eventually concluded.)

The company's initial business plan was to build space robots, an idea that can be traced back to Greiner's childhood in London. Greiner remembers being attracted to the field of robotics by the *Star Wars* films, and she imagined building robot companions like R2-D2. "At the time we started iRobot, there was lots of talk about commercial sponsorship of space flight, and we figured we would help to put robots on the moon." That plan, Greiner admits, "hasn't worked, and we had to put a stop to it if we intended to survive." But iRobot's three founders were convinced that their robots could also find a niche on earth.

They imagined free-range machines that would perform sophisticated tasks and react to their environment in an improvisational manner, much like living creatures. Robotics had already changed the automobile industry and other types of manufacturing—and those robots were bolted to the floor, designed to perform specialized and highly repetitive tasks. Greiner, Angle, and Brooks felt that robotics represented the next great growth industry, after the personal computer revolution.

"We knew that robotics was interesting and exciting," Brooks recalls. "But we didn't know what we were doing. We were just searching, searching, searching." Investors, who didn't believe that robots had much potential outside of the factory, were reluctant to back iRobot. "People ask how we funded ourselves. It was with my gold credit card," Brooks says. "It was tricky at times."

The company eventually built a small business around selling robots to university research labs, who would soup up iRobot's basic platform for their own experiments in free-range robotics. Some thirteen years later, the company has 110 employees, and offices in Massachusetts, New Hampshire, California, Hong Kong, and Washington, D.C. Venture capitalists have provided $20 million of funding.

The spectrum of projects iRobot has pursued is impressive: a custom-built robot called the Pyramid Rover, which starred in a *National Geographic* documentary, poking its fiber-optic camera into some long-forgotten chambers of the pyramids at Giza; the Roomba Robotic FloorVac, a roving vacuum cleaner sold in retail stores and catalogues that looks like a silver-domed room-service plate; and a rugged exploration robot called PackBot (it fits in a backpack), which U.S. Army troops have used on reconnaissance missions in Afghanistan and Iraq.

The company's headquarters have an atmosphere that is common to many start-ups. It feels like an amalgam of a playground, academic research lab, cubicle farm, and home away from home for a lot of young employees. As Greiner leads me through the offices and open work areas, she cheerfully points out an employee's pet gecko that has been named after her.

For a few minutes of the tour, Greiner is stalked by a small, tank-like PackBot. First, she waves to its camera, then she places a string of her Mardi Gras beads atop it; finally she tries to figure out who is giving the robot its marching orders. Reflecting on her company, Greiner says, "In the past, when we used to say 'we're worried about the future,' it meant, will we go out of business next month? Now it means, do we have the right vision for the future, the right products. This is a company that is creating an industry, not trying to invent something that is twenty percent better than a product that's out there. We need to keep doing research."

In one corner of the iRobot offices, an MIT doctoral student named James McLurkin is overseeing a project to develop software that will help robots work together in large groups. The research is being funded by DARPA (the Defense Advanced Research Projects Agency), the same arm of the Pentagon that hired Bolt, Beranek and Newman to assemble the first pieces of the Internet. The experiment looks like a demolition derby in miniature, sans metal-crunching collisions. Inside a low barrier of linked Styrofoam panels, about thirty robots scoot around on thirty different trajectories. The robots —McLurkin refers to them as Swarmbots—are five-inch-high cubes with indicator lights on top and wheels underneath. Each one is identical and loaded with the same software. A blue light flashes when they encounter a wall. When a green light flashes, it means the robot is low on battery power, and the robot begins communicating with its brethren, asking them where the recharging dock is located. When a robot gets separated from the group and can no longer talk to the others, it makes a distressed bonking sound.

"Imagine if somebody gave you ten thousand robots," McLurkin says. "How would you program them? Would you say, 'Robot number twenty-five, do this'? That's never going to work. You need to figure out ways to program the entire group as a whole. We're developing these behavioral building blocks. You can have them cluster around a suspicious object, or tell them to disperse and map an area." Much of McLurkin's swarming software is inspired by the way ants collaborate to find food.

While the sci-fi notion of swarming robots may sound alarming, these robots could prove extremely helpful in search-and-rescue operations following a natural (or man-made) disaster; after the attack on the World Trade Center, iRobot brought a PackBot to the site to search for survivors. But that was one robot, guided by one human. A team of thirty or more robots working as a swarm could cover more ground, more rapidly.

McLurkin and two colleagues stand over the robot pen, watching their experiment play out. The Swarmbots are finding walls and blinking blue, making a map of their world. (Occasionally, they have been known to break through the Styrofoam barrier and begin exploring the far reaches of the office, perhaps planning a rendezvous with the coffeemaker.) It's a basic behavior, but it is also a metaphor for the work of companies like iRobot, feeling for the bounds of what has already been accomplished and pushing past them. One Swarmbot starts to glow green and staggers back toward its U-shaped recharging dock. "I don't think he's going to make it," Greiner says, anthropomorphizing a device that looks like a mobile box of Kleenex. The robot falters and seems to peter out a few feet away from the dock. But then it locates a last reserve of energy and makes it in.

*  *  *

The elements that make up Boston's technology ecosystem are easy enough to enumerate, and they have not changed much from the time of Edison and Bell. There are the world-class universities of Boston that lure students and professors from all over, and then marinate them in corporate and government research dollars. When students graduate and want to start new companies, Boston's sharp-eyed venture capitalists provide funding and guidance and introduce young scientists to experienced executives who can help them manage and nurture their promising start-ups. There is a corps of skillful patent attorneys in town to help innovators protect their ideas. Not least, there are adventurous customers in the Boston metropolis, organizations willing to take a flier on new technologies. For software and hardware start-ups, there are large companies like Fidelity Investments, Staples, and Gillette that are constantly looking for technologies that will afford them an advantage in the marketplace. For companies developing new medical devices and drugs, there are a host of leading-edge hospitals in and around Boston.

Less easy is outlining how the Boston technology ecosystem can be replicated elsewhere. Foreign countries and other regions of the United States regularly send delegations of economic development officials to Boston to try to understand just what it is about the environment here that creates such fertile conditions for start-up companies.

Henri Termeer, the chief executive of Genzyme, Massachusetts' largest biotech firm, often meets with visiting dignitaries who want to know how they can cultivate, in their home state or country, the same high concentration of biotech companies that exists in the

Kendall Square area of Cambridge, located at the eastern border of the MIT campus. Termeer, who was born in the Netherlands, left a stable job at California-based Baxter International in 1983 to become CEO of the fledgling Genzyme. At that point, the MIT spin-off was just over a year old and its eleven employees were working with the National Institutes of Health on a therapeutic approach for rare diseases, an approach called enzyme replacement.

The company was tiny then, and Termeer and the other employees came to know the first patient to be treated with Genzyme's first product, a three-year-old boy who was suffering from Gaucher's disease, a serious metabolic disorder. With obvious satisfaction, Termeer reports that Patient no. 1 is still alive today, married with children. As Genzyme grew, Termeer led the company through an initial public offering, and today he oversees an enterprise that employs more than five thousand people and has revenues of more than $1 billion.

One morning, I went to see Termeer in his penthouse office atop Genzyme's shimmering new headquarters in Kendall Square. The company had only recently moved into the building, which is Boston's first major exemplar of "green architecture"—a forward-thinking approach to design and construction that places a premium on energy conservation and the use of natural light. The glass-walled building resembled a cubist interpretation of the Emerald City from *The Wizard of Oz*. On a round table in Termeer's office sat a glass vase of pink and yellow tulips.

Plenty of cities, Termeer reflected, wish they could find a way to foster more innovation and start-up activity. But some places are luckier than others. "The universities were here, the science was being developed here, and the venture capitalists were here," he said, explaining why Boston, along with San Francisco, became one of the country's biotech centers. "The explanation [for why some regions attract more innovation] is as simple as why you don't get tulip bulbs to grow in Russia," Termeer continued. "The soil is not there. Holland is a tiny country. Sixteen million people squeezed into a tiny piece of land, which is mostly below sea level. And they control the world market for bulbs. You can wish it, but if you don't have the soil, the history, the educational system, and the assumptions people make about the way their careers will go, all you will do is wish."

*   *   *

An unusual kind of recycling program also helps keep the Boston innovation economy humming. Entrepreneurs and technologists move from one company to another when lucrative opportunities beckon. An established company falters and its employees pollinate other companies in neighboring fields. Founders leave a successful start-up and join venture capital firms.

Buildings and equipment are recycled, too. The former Boott Cotton Mills facility in Lowell, near the New Hampshire border, is like a brick fortress surrounded by a moat. It was once a showcase of advanced factory equipment powered by water, steam, and, later, electricity. Lowell itself was long a center of the American textile industry, until production shifted to the South. Closed in 1955, the Boott Cotton Mills building now houses a museum of the industrial revolution—and several floors of reconditioned office space, with big arched windows, well-worn wood floors, and beamed ceilings.

One of the companies now housed in the old mill building is Konarka Technologies. Among other things, Konarka is working on a new kind of textile—a fiber capable of generating power from the sun. Woven into a parka, Konarka's solar-powered fiber would generate power to keep a skier's digital music player going all day long; an aid worker hiking into a remote village could rely on her backpack to keep her satellite phone fully charged.

"This was once the largest textile mill in the world, and it was powered by water—renewable energy," says Howard Berke, Konarka's chairman. "Now we are working on a new kind of textile that will use a different kind of renewable energy. Wait a hundred years, and things come full circle." In the 1990s Berke was working with administrators and professors at the University of Massachusetts' Lowell campus to start a business incubator that would support spin-offs from the school. In the process, he met a chemistry professor named Sukant Tripathy, who had been working for a decade on a method for "printing" solar cells onto plastic, which would make them lighter, more flexible, and less expensive than existing solar cells. Berke and Tripathy began talking about starting a company together. Tripathy had grown up in a rural Indian village called Bihar, and his vision was a power source that could bring inexpensive, clean electricity to the developing world.

A month before the planned launch of Konarka, Tripathy attended a chemistry conference in Hawaii. He went for a swim, was caught in a powerful riptide, and drowned. He was forty-eight. At first, Berke questioned whether he could continue without Tripathy, who had single-handedly laid the company's scientific foundation, but Tripathy's colleagues and former students rallied around the effort, and Tripathy's widow, encouraging Berke to go forward, supplied the company's name. One of Tripathy's favorite places in India was a temple called Konarka, dedicated to the god of the sun.

The company is a prime example of how recycling works. In 2002 Konarka moved into office space at the Boott Cotton Mills. The space had previously housed a company called Mission Critical Linux, which had laid off most of its staff. Konarka purchased some of Mission Critical's assets at an auction, including office furniture and a phone system. Several Konarka employees, including Russell Gaudiana, vice president of research and development, came from Polaroid (which was soon to file for bankruptcy protection). They advised Konarka to purchase certain pieces of surplus Polaroid equipment for ten cents on the dollar, and indeed Konarka now uses old Polaroid equipment for printing its flexible solar cells on plastic. The mill, the office space, the employees, and much of the equipment inside have all been recycled.

The equipment looks much like a printing press, or the inside of a movie projector, with spools that carry along an endless ribbon of plastic. Titanium dioxide (the substance that makes white paint white) is deposited on the plastic, followed by a dye and an electrolyte solution. Another layer of plastic is affixed to the top, creating a sandwich that generates electricity from the sun. Berke imagines the company's solar cells built into the backs of cell phones, laptops, and handheld computers. When the company's solar fiber is further along, it may be woven into drapes that would generate the power to open and close on their own.

Eventually, Berke says, if Konarka's plastic solar cells can be produced cheaply enough, they will make solar power competitive with electricity produced by centralized power plants. "At one dollar a watt, photovoltaic power will be competitive with grid electricity produced by fossil fuels," Berke says. "Before, without subsidies, it could never compete. Think of the roof of a Wal-Mart or Home Depot being used to produce power for the store, and feeding the excess into the grid."

What Berke and his colleagues don't talk about as much anymore is bringing solar power to the developing world. It is not that they have forgotten about Professor Tripathy's original objective. It's just that once a company accepts money from outside investors—and Konarka has collected about $15 million—the investors prod the company to chase known markets, customers with deep pockets. To investors, bringing solar power to rural villages sounds like a job for UNESCO.

Or possibly, that kind of work, on behalf of humankind and the health of the planet, is a job for a cluster of so-called developmental entrepreneurs based in Cambridge who are coming up with new strategies for getting innovations to the places where they are needed most. Nitin Sawhney, one of the leaders of this charge, is an Indian-born engineer who grew up in Iran and Bahrain. Sawhney came to Massachusetts to get a doctoral degree at MIT's famed Media Lab. One of his first projects there was a device called the nomadic radio. Users wore it like a necklace, and it would play customized news reports, read incoming e-mail, and notify the wearer of upcoming meetings.

"This is interesting," Sawhney thought after he had crafted a prototype, "but what I'm building is a toy for rich people." Banding together with several other students at the Media Lab, Sawhney started ThinkCycle, an organization whose objective was to get engineers like Sawhney and his friends focused on problems in the developing world, rather than flashy new technologies for affluent consumers. "All of us had some experience in developing countries, and all of us felt some level of agony over not being able to take our research and see what kinds of impacts it might have there," Sawhney says over coffee at a Harvard Square café.

Before long, the group had started a student club at MIT called Design That Matters, and had devised two courses on solving technology problems in the developing world. The ThinkCycle Web site features a database of problems submitted by various nongovernmental organizations around the world, which serve as the basis for student engineering projects at MIT and elsewhere. Already, students have come up with inventions like a machine that can produce eyeglasses at very low cost; an incubator that doesn't require electricity to keep infants warm; and inexpensive water-filtration technologies. Versions of the original MIT Design That Matters course are now taught in Portugal, Kenya, Brazil, and India, creating what Sawhney calls a global design network. "The idea is to continually keep people thinking," Sawhney says. "What are some of the problems out there in the world, and how can engineering students come up with simple solutions?"

* * *

Bostonians often look west to Silicon Valley and wonder whether denizens of that region know something we don't. The Boston area does well at bringing technologies out of the lab and into the marketplace, but it doesn't seem able to spawn industry giants like Intel, Apple, Oracle, and eBay as readily as the Valley. Only a handful of the companies in the Nasdaq 100 are based in Massachusetts; the vast majority are rooted in California.

California venture capitalists are painted as more adventurous than their Massachusetts counterparts. (One story I was told, during the height of the Internet frenzy, involved a Boston-area entrepreneur who signed an agreement with his Silicon Valley investors on the trunk of a car, after an intense game of Ultimate Frisbee.) Valley entrepreneurs are purported to spend more time schmoozing with colleagues in the industry. The burritos—that staple food of late-night work sessions—are empirically better out West.

Rarely do Boston companies acquire rivals in San Francisco. More often, West Coast players snap up Massachusetts firms. (On the bright side, West Coast tech concerns often establish R & D outposts and engineering offices here, and the pharmaceutical giants Merck and Novartis have decided to locate major R & D labs in Cambridge.) That dynamic sometimes gives Boston techies the feeling that they are playing for a farm team rather than the major leagues.

"I think that Boston and the Bay Area are on equal footing in terms of creativeness and inventiveness," says Howard Berke, who has managed companies on both coasts. "But in Boston, invention is more revered. We appreciate academic pursuits here. In Silicon Valley, commercial success is what is prized. There's more of a compulsion to dominate and crush, to play to win, to gather all the chips."

Berke is right, I think, but more specifically, what Boston lacks is a deep bench of executive talent; it is rare here to find an experienced technology CEO who can grow a billion-dollar company and ensure that it retains its edge as customers' needs change and competitors' products get better. (This problem is less pronounced in the biotech field.) Executives who want to run large, publicly held tech companies gravitate to the Valley, because that is where the best opportunities lie. Where does that leave Boston?

"Boston has an ability to keep creating waves of innovation," says Bob Krim, executive director of the Boston History Collaborative. Krim helped assemble a tour called the Innovation Odyssey, a tech-oriented alternative to the Freedom Trail, which passes sites like 109 Court Street and the Ether Dome at Massachusetts General Hospital, where general anesthesia was first administered. (Krim's father, as it happens, was one of the Raytheon engineers who contributed to the radar and communications technologies that helped the Allies win World War II.)

"People worry when one industry starts to wane," Krim says, "whether it's the shoe industry or the textile industry or the minicomputer industry, but Boston has this infrastructure of innovation that's very powerful. The city has a very good ability to be in a strong position in each successive wave."

The people attracted to Boston seem to gauge their progress not by how high their company has climbed on the Fortune 500 list. Instead, what matters is where their last big idea registers on the Richter scale. Does it rattle the bone china of tradition and rearrange the tectonic plates of established industries?

There's a persistence of innovation here that feels like a geological force—inexorable, by turns constructive and destructive. Boston was a center for telegraphic technology when Thomas Edison and Alexander Graham Bell rented lab space from Charles Williams. That once-vibrant industry crumbled, supplanted by the telephone. A century and a half later, Boston is home to companies that are working on enhancements (and replacements) for the telephone—the microchips that power cell phones, videoconferencing systems, speech-recognition software that allows you to call an 800 number and plan your next Amtrak trip with a virtual agent.

Inside a drug discovery lab at Genzyme, I met a staff scientist named Jill Gregory. Gregory showed me a test she was performing. She was looking for chemical compounds—drugs, in their crudest form—that can kill cysts in a person's kidney. Gregory held a plastic tray about the size of an index card that was dotted with ninety-six wells, or little divots. Inside each well, chemical compounds and samples of cystic kidney cells would be deposited by a machine. "We're looking for compounds that kill cysts, but we don't want them to kill normal kidney cells," Gregory explained. "If the well hits, that's exciting," she says, sounding a bit like a Texas wildcatter.

Gregory has been working at Genzyme for eight years. She has performed tens of thousands of tests with trays like this one, using a library of 3 million different chemical compounds, each of which might successfully combat a particular aspect of a particular disease. So far, Gregory has found exactly one compound that evolved into a drug and has made it as far as clinical trials in humans, which began in late 2003. It was dubbed GENZ 29155, and Genzyme hopes that it will help those suffering from multiple sclerosis. "My job is like walking along the beach, looking for a piece of gold," Gregory says. "The likelihood that you are going to find it might be low, but you can't stop looking for it. I like sifting, the idea that I have three million things, and you can look at all different kinds of [disease] targets. It's like a treasure hunt. Fifty years ago, polio and smallpox were major things. I'd like to come back in one hundred years and see how much we know. Everything we're obsessed with now will be so obvious."

By then, the building in which Gregory works may be gone. If it endures, it may be listed as a historic landmark and occupied by another researcher sifting through millions of possibilities, seeking a solution to some as-yet-unsolved problem. In Boston, buildings rise and fall, but this restless pursuit of the next breakthrough never seems to wane. Part of the secret, the reason Boston has produced bumper crop after bumper crop of important new technologies, may lie in the soil, as Henri Termeer suggests. But there is also a constructive tension between Establishment Boston—the city of venerable banks, law firms, and universities—and Upstart Boston. Establishment Boston prizes tradition and stability. Upstart Boston huddles in cheap office space, in places like 109 Court Street, cultivating nontraditional ideas that threaten to destabilize the establishment. Boston is a city that attracts people who want to work in industries that have existed here since Massachusetts was a British colony. It is also the city for those who believe that the only industry worth working in is the one they're about to create.

# A Mixing Chamber

*Robert Campbell*

Boston is a city, and the virtues of cities are very different from the virtues of suburbs or rural areas. One of those virtues is density—in other words, a lot of people living and working near one another. Americans, going back to Jefferson and his vision of a rural nation, tend to have a bias against density. But congestion and density are not necessarily bad qualities in a city. The very definition of a city is that it is a place with a relatively high density of population. And indeed, when we vote with our feet instead of our words, it turns out that the places of highest density often turn out to be the most desirable, at least if you measure desirability by the high cost of dwelling. Think of the Upper East Side of Manhattan or New York neighborhoods like Tribeca. American slums, by contrast, are invariably low-density areas. In cities, density attracts and emptiness repels.

Boston, then, should be proud of being one of the most densely populated American cities. Even so, it is thin compared to the rest of the world. Paris, for instance, has roughly the same area as Boston (we're speaking of Paris proper and Boston proper, not the metro areas). But Paris packs in more than four times as many people as Boston. It does that with almost no high-rise buildings, and with lots of parks and boulevards. So density doesn't necessarily mean overwhelming scale. The density of Paris is what supports all those streets with continuous shopping, not to mention the Metro, with its 270 stops.

Nor does density mean traffic problems. I remember once the planning director of Copenhagen saying, "We need to increase density in order to reduce traffic." And indeed, as everyone knows, the worst traffic problems in the Boston area occur in the thinly populated, spread-out towns along the Route 128 corridor—not in Boston, nor in the inner metropolitan communities like Cambridge or Somerville, which, according to one study, happen to be the two most densely populated cities in the United States outside of the New York metro area. What causes traffic is the number and length of car trips, not the density of population, and it is in the suburbs that the most frequent and longest rides are necessary, just because everything is sited so far from everything else.

So what are the virtues of density? Any Bostonian can tell you, and the great urbanist Lewis Mumford said it best. He wrote that a city is the place where, in the smallest possible area, you have the greatest possible variety of choice—social, moral, commercial, every kind of choice. Note the words "smallest possible area." Maximizing choice in a small area means mixing all kinds of people and uses together, not zoning the city for rich residents here and office parks there.

The city, most of all, is the place of accidental encounter. Accidental encounters happen when you walk, not when you travel in your sealed car. In Boston things are close enough together that you can walk from one to another. As you do, surprises begin to happen. You run unexpectedly into friends. Or you're seduced by a bookstore window. Or you notice for the first time a choice work of architecture. Or you stop to watch a bocce game. City life, in that sense, is unpredictable.

I remember the movie *Searching for Bobby Fischer* some years ago, where a little kid in New York is taken regularly by his mother to Washington Square Park. He becomes fascinated by the outdoor chess players there, and develops into a chess champion himself. I've always thought this was the metaphor for the city: the place where you encounter other kinds of people and other kinds of interests from the ones you're used to, and where, as a result, you are stimulated and you grow. Life is richer for being less predictable. We all know there are risks in unpredictability. Not every encounter will be a pleasant one. But risks must be taken if life is to be fully lived.

Boston, like any city, is a crucible of democracy, a mixing chamber. Here we encounter and come to know our fellow citizens of every economic and social group. We learn to empathize with one another's problems. And we therefore learn to act and vote in a way that benefits the entire community and not merely our own private interests. Boston is not perfect. We have a long way to go before we achieve an optimal democracy. But when you compare our city to the typical development patterns of other regions in recent decades, where different ethnic and economic groups are so often rigidly divided into separate gated enclaves, we look pretty good.

The longer Boston can retain its true city character—as a dense, exciting place where lots of different things and people bump into one another unpredictably within a framework of streets and buildings of a human scale—the more precious this city will become.

# On Location: Place and Politics in a Changing City

*Jane Holtz Kay*

I grew up in politics, I always say, as if politics were a place: the Republic of Angst and Laughter, the City of Empty (or Leaky) Purses. In Boston, politics is a local sport, but the game is always beached in place, in the physical surroundings of the city: in the neighborhoods, the splendid buildings, the elegant parks. Navigating the city's close-packed streets, politicians practiced a door-to-door campaign style in my youth, and the habit has endured. Despite the election-day messages that clog my phone wires and the media-hyping on TV, Boston's walkable, livable next-doorness defines our politics.

More than any other city in America, the core of Boston—"the Hub," as the nineteenth-century author Oliver Wendell Holmes nicknamed it, short for "hub of the solar system"—still survives as the heart of the modern city. Geographically, culturally, and intellectually, hub remains the right image for the core city—conveying the fact that our schools, our hospitals, our think tanks, political structures, and universities are within walking, or streetcar, distance from the original "city upon a hill." That name and idea for the city— applied by John Winthrop, the founding Puritan father, who defined both his theological aspirations and the literal city atop the most prominent hill of the Shawmut Peninsula—have lingered into the twenty-first century.

Both the reigning state and city governments lie within a half-mile walk of each other. To this day, our state government remains where it was born, generations ago, in the State House under Bulfinch's golden dome. Nearby, our nineteenth-century Old City Hall designed by Bryant and Gilman is intact. To the east our *new* City Hall, designed by Kallmann, McKinnell, and Knowles, also lies within the radius of the State House, less than a five-minute walk away from its predecessor.

Only Providence, Rhode Island, boasts the same proximity between its domed State House and City Hall, and an urban core. Elsewhere, the capitols of America's states reside far from the heart of the cities whose fate they often decide with cavalier indifference. Remote from urban sensibilities, the legislators in these government outlands are prone to vote for policies that fund and subsidize the flight to the suburbs. Their planning—developer driven, car friendly, and invasive—uproots citizens from downtowns and moves them to the fringes of the metropolis via the massive highways that undercut urban life.

* * *

As a child of the city, a reader of its history, and a daughter of a Boston lawyer and politician, I see profound links between our walkable, urban landscape and the history that we Bostonians guard. So do countless activists and organizations that dote on this city, fret about the failure of urban federal policies, and deplore poor local planning to stop the exodus to distant enclaves. They watch with alarm as the mounting traffic and the form and function of the massive buildings defile Boston's human scale and noble past. Outside the compact core and streetcar suburbs, sprawl takes hold. We sadly watch our state's growing share of the nation's new rambling developments (from ranchettes to starter castles, some 16 million a year) draining the cities. We deplore our officialdom that rolls out the financial welcome mat to ever more hardtop to swell our share of the nation's 17 million new cars per year—roads and cars that undermine the public transportation that holds a citizenry together and creates a pedestrian environment. Good planning is the agent of good living, history teaches us, and we forget it to our sorrow.

Here lie the reasons that Boston Democrats and city aficionados everywhere voted for Al Gore through political habit (not to mention fear of the Republican nominee's urban/environmental malice). Visible before Bush rode his hobbyhorse into the White House, the forty-third president's "that's our oil under your soil" style of governance makes us tremble, and rightly so; it is an affront to all who care—and understand—how sustainable, livable cities thrive.

In Boston, our citizens know that Boston proper, the core of the city, is the soul and source for the entire metropolis. And this comprehension goes beyond mere chauvinism. For the city of Boston functions as a model of our national identity. America the nation looks to Boston as a well of historical meaning, of worldly and spiritual wealth, a place that tells us just who we are as Americans. Regionally, too, the surrounding communities look to Boston as the financial, intellectual, and political core. Despite the dispersal of metropolitan citizens to the beauteous suburbs, the municipality is still a hub-and-spokes city.

It is the vitality of that central city that catalyzes "Main Street" makeover programs in newly enhanced neighborhoods like Southie (South Boston), Jamaica Plain, and Roslindale: makeovers that have turned dreary fringes of the city into somewheres, reviving once downtrodden subcities into cozy emporiums of the ethnic, the chic, the helpful, the everyday. And the inhabitants of these metropolitan villages remain proudly urban.

The city's neighborhoods, home to clusters of (ever changing) ethnic and racial groups, are linked to the Hub not only by proximity and history but by their literal annexation to the city at the turn of the century. As modern engineering advanced, Boston began to lure surrounding towns to share its governance by offering the new services of water, electricity, and sewage treatment. Today in these subcities, the vaunted politics of neighborhoods, the edgy ethnicity, the fractiousness of racial diversity and shaky finances, still endure . . .

along with pride in the revival of the handsome old housing stock. Still, for all the centrality of this city, and its uptick in urban housing, more-distant towns have sidled away from Boston's metropolis and its web of mobility by streetcar, bus, and commuter rail. Spreading to the hinterlands, the newcomers and former urbanites unwittingly destroy the rural sense of place they inhabit, swelling the crowded highways as they commute to work.

*  *  *

A number of years ago, the publisher of a series on lost cities asked me, "Is there enough to write a book on Boston?" My answer came back quickly.

"Why, yes," I responded in short order. "Boston has lost more than anyone," and the book I wrote, *Lost Boston*, documented some three hundred places that had indeed vanished. "*Boston lost?*" How depressing, friends and colleagues repeated when the book appeared, bulging with images of the old city now gone. "No," I replied, "Boston isn't lost: It's old, it's here, it's ours; it's evolving."

My friends were right, of course, and so was I. For Boston, as it went through its eras of expansion and replacement in earlier centuries, managed to lose yet gain with the loss: the splendid eighteenth-century mansions were replaced by magnificent nineteenth-century row houses. A fine landscape, rich with species and waterways at the Puritan landing, shaped and made the new a fine proxy for the old in terms of aesthetics and design. Boston in the twentieth and opening years of the twenty-first centuries has, alas, done otherwise.

Post–World War II America was hardly a time when permanence was the nation's most important product. The political, social, and economic passion for the new was played out everywhere, including Boston. "The United States from 1930 to 1970—when most of us were youths—was a nation of big projects: high dams, soaring bridges, miles of interstate highways," the editor of *Trains* magazine summed it up. Building the big destroyed the little, the intimate, the eternal that we cherished.

For me and many others, the most painful experience was the loss of Boston's West End, destroyed during the era of urban renewal in the 1950s. The West End was the site of my grandparents' home, the neighborhood where my father grew up, and a place of many memories. Although my sister and I were raised in Dorchester and Brookline, we knew the neighborhood well when we were young, and later I worked in a nearby flower shop on Christmas breaks during college. When the West End was demolished—despite the labors of my father and others to defend it—the city, our family, and seven thousand West Enders lost a beloved community. The lives of residents and storekeepers of many nationalities were destroyed in favor of luxury apartments and government buildings, as urban renewers played cozy with developers whose pockets were deeper than their values.

Still, the essence of Boston endures amid catastrophe and change. Pass through the superb Boston Public Library by McKim, Mead, and White on Copley Square, stop by its John Singer Sargent murals, visit the Isabella Stewart Gardner Museum or the Museum of Fine Arts. Such Boston moments compress the centuries and pass for an eternity in instantaneous America. Check out a book at the Boston Athenaeum's private library; and if you're lucky, you may find a card bearing the signature of a 1940 borrower. Visit Old North Church, the gorgeous brick neighborhoods, the Public Garden. The list is endless.

\*   \*   \*

Transformation and expansion have always characterized this historic city. The first Europeans to arrive on the Shawmut Peninsula saw a trio of hills—Beacon, Copps, and Fort. No sooner had John Winthrop and his flock arrived in 1630 than the acts of flattening his vaunted city upon a hill to fill and build began. The same missionary zeal characterized the actions of later settlers, who would decapitate the hills to fill wetlands, making new land for wharves, churches, and dwellings. By wharfing out and filling marsh (as they would for centuries), Bostonians tripled our city's land mass—from 843 acres (about the size of Central Park) to 2,100 acres, according to tradition, though lately the estimate grows to 5,200 acres.

The new Bostonians also prospered. Like Caesar, who found Rome in brick and left it in marble, the builders of the Shawmut

Peninsula settled the town in baled straw huts, hardened it in wood, laid it in brick, and carved symbols of granite and marble to reflect their power and glory over time.

As the population grew, the waterbound soil was sponged with still more earth. In the South End, some 570 acres of the former tidal flats were filled to allow the creation of the splendid oval-centered streets, modeled on those in England. Not long thereafter, the east-west axis from downtown to the setting sun became the more prosperous site for Back Bay builders. Importing Parisian design, this time from Baron Haussmann's grand boulevard, and scooping Needham's soil for landfill of the mudflats, builders gradually created the magnificent progression of row houses for city dwellers and their ecclesiastical and educational institutions.

In the summer, Boston baked in the warm weather. Muggy days sent the city's elite to country houses in Roxbury Highlands or Brookline, close to home, or to points north along the coast. Soon, however, the enticement of waterworks, streetcars, and modern facilities drew a more permanent population to the new suburbs as the city lured Jamaica Plain, Roslindale, West Roxbury (and later Hyde Park) to formally join the urban core. Only Brookline opted out of the city's bid for annexation.

Boston achieved its greatest horticultural coup by attracting the green prince of landscape, the creator of Central Park and founder of what we now call urban ecology, when Frederick Law Olmsted took up the task of making over Boston's landscape. Stewardship was not even a thought during the earliest conversions of the Shawmut Peninsula. And in the flow of time, the city bore the price in the stench and degradation of the waterways throughout the metropolis. To remedy matters, Bostonians invited Olmsted to remake the local landscape. And so he did, creating our premier approach to "design with nature." Settling in Brookline at the invitation of H. H. Richardson, the architect of Trinity Church, Olmsted created an "Emerald Necklace" of greenswards and blue waters to restore the land corrupted by heroic building. In the end, the necklace wrapped around the Muddy River and the Fens, working its way to the Arnold Arboretum and culminating in Olmsted's masterwork, Franklin Park.

\*   \*   \*

Will this legacy of good design and public planning endure or vanish in today's Boston? Can the old city upon a hill have a gold standard of planning in a nation that follows the whims of would-be gilded developers? Yes, the Hub's landscape thrives. Neighborhoods revive, buildings rise. We have a boom.

Yet the close-packed plan that made Boston a walkable gem of a city is assaulted by today's developers. High-rises soar above the human-scaled city. Their churning winds assail walkers and darken whole neighborhoods in their shadow. Below, their cavernous garages create gaps that intercept the sidewalk. As budgets shrink, the search for affordable housing loses allies and Boston's splendid park system lacks a commissioner and custodial care.

Privatism also swells as owners restrict access to their views of the sea, closing off precious vistas. Faceless corporate constructors like Marriott closed off, then opened, then virtually obliterated, access to the Custom House Tower balcony view near Quincy Market; John Hancock's top-floor viewing post was unceremoniously shut down (as is the company now). And, more profoundly and immediately, in the new outpost of land at the South Boston seaport, the 125-acre site that includes the convention hall offers little planning and less public participation. The old, carefully wrought public-planning process caves in to the whims of developers and mandates from authorities like Massport and Masspike, powerbrokers in the auto-air age.

Is Boston living on its legacy? Yes, and splendidly, I think, but we need to do more. Much more. Happily, we downed the Central Artery with the $14.5 billion Big Dig: A heroic improvement, in the mode of history's great remakes. But what will be *its* legacy? We will have the open swath of land with sky above, but what will we build there? Lacking leadership, designers, and public funds, the lessons of history will hopefully help us devise a plan.

The art of planning and the art of politics are fused in Boston. Engaged, passionate, active citizens remain. Together, they are Boston's last best hope, as they are the country's. A nation that is losing the health of its biological systems and the wealth of its cities day by day must reinforce itself through science, art, and politics. I and my friends and colleagues struggle. My officemate keeps what she calls a "curmudgeon file," listing the downed, and near-downed, buildings, and I consult with her for the correct information on the Northern Avenue Bridge crossing from Boston over the Fort Point Channel to the new seaport land.

Another friend fumes about the old buildings' lobbies with their passageways that once let pedestrians scoot from building to building, skirting the cold, but now—post-9/11—are blocked off. The privatization is typical, the power of developers with deep pockets persistent. But so is the political activism of those who resist and have lived through campaigns and causes a'plenty. They hold out hope, as they always have: For to grow up in this place is not only to inhabit a landscape, but a state of mind and a motif for action.

*   *   *

On my walk home from work, I pass a sign that marks the site, a shoe store on Court Street, where evangelist Dwight Moody saw the light, just paces from Ben Franklin's printing shop. On my own street, too, I see a plaque on a brick row-house wall that honors Harriet Hemenway, the turn-of-the-twentieth-century crusader who took her ire about the feathered hats of her neighbors—a fashion then decimating America's birds—and began the campaign that inspired creation of the Massachusetts Audubon Society. Hemenway is, I confess, my heroine, and I see her legacy elsewhere too, in Boston's citizenry.

Just this winter, the Audubon Society sounded an alarm for the state of our region, releasing the news that forty acres are dying daily in the Bay State, that land is being deprived of its biological diversity by highway-based development and driven to extinction by sprawl. "Sprawl," that word of dubious etymology and recent birth, is the enemy as we try to create civilized cities. And, however else we deal with our political lives, those who relish this still livable city and care to steward their own space on this fragile, battered planet, might retain Boston's new/old model of location: An ever changing, ever enduring city where good politics and a good sense of planning embrace to create an everlasting union of the bygone and the still beginning.

# An Intimate Geography:
# Boston Neighborhoods

*Lynda Morgenroth*

Neighborhood" is one of those simple, complicated words like "marriage" or "dog" or "friend." We all know what a marriage is, or a dog. But for anyone who has ever been married, or had a dog or a friend or other close attachments, these are words with personal, idiosyncratic, individual meanings. The older we are—the more marriages, dogs, and friends we have had, and the more neighborhoods we have lived in—the more layered and intermingled these relationships become.

Our neighborhoods are as vivid and influential as our houses, apartments, and rooms. They help to shape us; providing stages, characters, and props, not to mention material and dialogue. Our arrivals and departures from these intimate geographies mark phases of our lives. These places not only form, but store, experiences and events, our former and formative selves, and the parts of life we shared with others.

A neighborhood post office staffed by wisecracking, muttonchop-wearing Vietnam vets, with rock music blaring (Stuart Street in the

Back Bay), and a tiny, tidy post office, quiet as a library, with potted plants in winter windows (Charles Street on Beacon Hill) can cause flashback in longtime residents who leave and return for stamps and more.

I have lived in Boston for over thirty years, arriving in this city during the 1960s as a hopeful college student, and staying on through seasons of discovery, discontent, and perennial reevaluation, as my hair changed from glossy dark brown to white. During those years, I migrated from neighborhood to neighborhood, and have lived, variously, in the most elegant part of the Back Bay, on a funky side street in Allston, on a leafy terrace in Brookline, and for many years in apartments and houses across the river from Boston proper, in Cambridge between Harvard and Porter Squares. Two different boyfriends lived in Jamaica Plain, which caused me to frequent that bohemian quarter of the city, and a longtime flame occupied a trendy flat in the South End. Today, so many years after these emotional pageants played out, even a visit to the post office in one of these neighborhoods makes me shaky with emotion—a vestigial vibration of old romance.

I could take you to these neighborhoods, even to the memory-laden post offices (there are eight of them; I wrote a lot of letters), but I cannot show them to you exactly as I see them. Each of us forms his or her own idiosyncratic layers of memory and association when living in a place over time. And in Boston, both the fabled quarters and the more-secretive neighborhoods known only to residents lend themselves to the layering of varied, complicated, interesting lives. Like an oyster bed or an ocean reef, Boston's architecture and quirky street plans are textured, unpredictable, and distinctive. Here, our experiences cling to the city more thoroughly than they would in a place of smooth and regular surfaces.

If I had once quarreled with a lover in the parking lot of a mall, or on a flat, anonymous suburban street, the event would scarcely have had the drama of turning on my heel (high-heeled boot, actually) in Boston's theater district, running off into the night, then breaking my heel and twisting my ankle on the brick-paved streets of the Back Bay. That ankle, never fully healed, still throbs today when I pass the Shubert Theatre, or when I traverse some patch of old and irregular brick pavement. A bittersweet memory of a youthful and melodramatic quarrel, lingering, appropriately, in the city's theater district.

For years I took visitors into the Boston neighborhoods I knew best. I'd start out in a chipper, energetic frame of mind, but by day's end would feel curiously depleted. It wasn't that I was physically tired, although my guests and I did a lot of walking and talking. The cause of my fatigue, I came to realize, was mental; an overload of memory and associations with the places we'd visited. I felt like a character in a Viennese operetta. Too much had happened to me, and on such a small, continually revisited stage.

Historically, a place becomes a neighborhood because of its particularities of geography, history, architecture, and the ethnicities and occupations of its longtime residents. The atmosphere of an old, settled urban neighborhood is especially rich, promoting interaction and experience. (For what is experience, after all, other than the slow accretion of relationships, layer upon layer? Our relationships are with nature and God, with each other and animals, and with what people have created—buildings and parks, goods and services, paintings, music, and dance.)

\* \* \*

Like most cities, but more so, Boston is an aggregate of neighborhoods. When civic boosters and tourists speak of Boston, they generally mean the core city, the parts that became urbanized first—today's financial district and commercial downtown, the waterfront and Faneuil Hall Marketplace, the North End and Chinatown. Beacon Hill, site of the gold-domed State House and tony residential streets between the Charles River and Boston Common, are also part of the core, and the Back Bay, with its grand Commonwealth Avenue, Boston's Champs Élysées. The South End, a nineteenth-century neighborhood of row houses and English-style squares that preceded the development of the Back Bay, and which has been regentrified over the last two decades (freshly baked dog biscuits are now sold in the bakeries), is also part of this featured attraction.

This is the Boston that first appeals to visitors and newcomers.

With a cushy income, you might occupy the glittering city happily, sampling pizza, biscotti, and espresso in the North End, sushi, pad Thai, and lobster Cantonese in Chinatown, cod or scrod or even Dover sole all over town. You could eat cold oysters at the Union Oyster House, and warm, molasses-laden Indian pudding at Durgin Park, allowing the dollop of vanilla ice cream to semimelt on Boston's premier comfort food. You would have no need of a car, and could even eschew the T—choosing to stride across parks and malls, and to walk or jog along the Charles River, the harbor, the paths and rivulets of the Fens.

But if you are an urban wanderer, the type who will follow streets, paths, and alleyways because they are there, you will inevitably discover Boston's other, less obvious, neighborhoods. In addition to the Back Bay, Beacon Hill, the North End, and Chinatown, there are also neighborhoods called Mission Hill and Mattapan, Dorchester, Roxbury, and the Fenway, Jamaica Plain, Roslindale, and Hyde Park, Charlestown, East Boston, South Boston (different from the South End), Allston-Brighton, and more. All these places lie within the official boundaries of Boston.

The broad reach of the metropolis extends farther still; over the river to Cambridge, and along the old MBTA tracks to the "streetcar suburb" of Brookline, with its great shopping streets in Coolidge Corner, including a vintage shopping arcade. Watertown, along the Charles River, with bus connections to Cambridge, is home to a vibrant Armenian American community with Armenian churches, cultural centers, specialty bakeries, and groceries, with produce so fresh you can grow a living loquat from the pit of the fruit you buy.

Of all the Boston neighborhoods I have inhabited, the Back Bay has accumulated the most layers of personal association. (Perhaps its alluvial past lends itself to psychic accretion, as well as the piling up of physical muck). The formerly fetid wetland, filled between 1814 and the 1880s, is now the quintessential Boston neighborhood—a residential, commercial, and cultural hub. The district includes a portion of the Charles River and its recreational paths, the Public Garden and its pond, and the Commonwealth Avenue Mall. The city's fabled Emerald Necklace runs through the heart of the neighborhood. This linked chain of parklands designed by Frederick Law

Olmsted begins at Boston Common and the Public Garden, traverses the Back Bay along the greensward of the Commonwealth Avenue Mall, and extends on to the Fens, Riverway, Olmsted Park, Jamaica Pond, Arnold Arboretum, and vast Franklin Park in Jamaica Plain, Dorchester, and Roxbury.

The Back Bay even has its own common, or town square: majestic Copley Square, home to the Boston Public Library, Trinity Church, New Old South Church, the Copley Plaza Hotel, and insurance-company towers.

The street plan is a tidy grid. Commonwealth Avenue is the wide main boulevard, crossed by a series of alphabetically named streets — Arlington, Berkeley, Clarendon, Dartmouth, Exeter, Fairfield, Gloucester, Hereford. As you walk along the avenue, it is invigorating to consider the nineteenth-century Yankees who spun gold from dross, converting noxious tidal flats into this residential thoroughfare modeled on Parisian boulevards. Accounts of conditions in the pre-landfill days were detailed in letters from outraged citizens about the health menace and stench of the swamp, and the dead horses and other effluvia washed up on shores of the sluggish estuary, including by-products of unsuccessful outcomes at the Massachusetts General Hospital.

Dividing the commercial and residential sections of the Back Bay, Commonwealth Avenue runs parallel to Beacon and Boylston Streets. Beacon, one way outbound, which starts downtown near the State House, is primarily residential until Kenmore Square, while Boylston, one way inbound, is a glitzy, noisy street of banks, department stores, copy shops, and eyeglass emporiums. Located between Boylston and Commonwealth, Newbury Street is "fancy," with high-end boutiques, specialty stores, and the city's well-established art galleries, jewelry, and antique stores.

The neighborhood is like a miniature nation. To walk from brawny Boylston Street to sedate Newbury Street to residential Commonwealth Avenue is like going from the commercial city and town to the residential village. If you continue toward the Charles River, taking the Arthur Fiedler footbridge over Storrow Drive, you're in the country, following a river, especially in early morning when traffic is minimal.

As our personal experiences merge with the physical surroundings of our neighborhoods, we make a collage of memory, association, and place. This accumulation of incident happens wherever we are, even if we don't go out much, or live alone in a high-rise. The light on the walls comes in similarly but differently each day. Dust collects on a table in a pattern reflecting its use. Snow falls. The feathers of the sparrow we see through a window change color. One day there is weak, muted peeping from under an eave; soon the peeping becomes louder, insistent, raucous. Ice on the pond, or in the gutters, melts. A letter with handwriting we had forgotten, yet recognize, arrives.

I lived for over a decade on Commonwealth Avenue—Comm. Ave., as the boulevard is locally known. My friend Julie lived diagonally across the street, on the Comm. Ave./Clarendon Street corner facing First Baptist Church, an H. H. Richardson building, made of Roxbury puddingstone, with a frieze depicting the sacraments and, for good measure, trumpeting angels. (The frieze was designed by Bartholdi, sculptor of the Statue of Liberty.) I lived near the Comm. Ave./Berkeley Street corner adjacent to First and Second Church on Marlborough Street. At that time, Julie and I were each in our thirties, divorced, living with good men in long, committed relationships. We developed the custom of handwriting letters to each other and slipping them under the other's door. The letters were often accompanied by a small gift left on the stoop or behind a column—a book, a drawing, a bag of ginger scones. We both worked at home and relished being outdoors; we often met on the wide grassy mall, including for afternoon tea. Even in chilly April and November, we would gather on a bench. Julie would bring a thermos of hot tea, cloth napkins, and mugs. I would bring a plate of cookies, or cut-up cornbread with Vermont cheddar cheese. More than once, passersby asked where we had gotten our spread. Walking the green promenade of Commonwealth Avenue today, I still sense the two of us—our hopefulness, mainly—on late afternoons.

In those years, I worked out at the old brick YWCA nearby, "the girls' Y," located on Clarendon Street. The wind tunnel created by the adjacent John Hancock Tower could sweep smaller citizens into the street. I was several times slammed hard onto the hood of parked cars and into the arms of fellow pedestrians. (Once a man I was suddenly pressed against asked, "Would you like to dance?") At the Y in our noontime exercise class, I met Sylvia, my friend from Jamaica. Sylvia and I were the same age, same height, both vegetarians, both plant and animal lovers, and a mix of sociable and guarded. Sylvia had exquisite taste and dressed in fashionable clothing and accessories, including colorful draped silk scarves. She decorated her apartment with imposing, Edwardian-style furniture. For years we took crazy, probably injurious, classes, doing jerky aerobics to an instructor's scratchy boom-box tapes, working out in a majestic old wood-paneled room more like a boardroom than a gym. After class, Sylvia would walk with me toward my home, telling elaborate stories of her girlhood in Jamaica, speaking in a musical cadence. Her stories, almost songs, seemed to rise into the canopy of elm trees. We shared secrets about our families and marriages, bitterness and disappointment mixing with laughter, our take on life quite similar. When a story was sad, we sat on a bench and cried. We had come to Boston from very different places and yet we felt like sisters. The city had gathered us together.

My long, narrow, high-ceilinged study overlooking Commonwealth Avenue had one tall window, from which I could watch the seasonal pageant of the American elms that lined the mall. The graceful trees were so old, so enormous, that some branches touched the ground. Others arched across the pedestrian mall, over car traffic, parked cars, sidewalk, and entryway stairs, to brush my third-floor-study window. It was hard not to be a pantheist, the trees and I were so close. For fifteen years, I kept a daily vigil, looking down at the mall and up at the trees. In summer, I saw neighbors who watered the elms (all affected with Dutch-elm disease) carrying umpteen filled buckets across the busy street onto the parched mall where the elms lived, struggled, and died. Even spiffy bankers in pinstriped suits carried water to the elms, the water sloshing in pails and onto their pressed trousers and shiny shoes.

The veterans passed on Veterans' Day, old men in well-ironed uniforms, men my late father's age who had fought in World War II as he did, and younger men in jeans with beards, long hair, and caps—

the Woodstock soldiers, my generation; all carrying the American flag. Three times, blizzards totally covered the parked cars, meters, hydrants, and mailboxes, transforming the neighborhood into its nineteenth-century self.

From my rear bedroom, a round room with pocket doors and falling plaster, I could view the colorfully clad children in the First and Second Church daycare. Many were toddlers, and swirled into motion and screamed with delight in the courtyard, and sometimes, apropos of nothing, bopped each other on the head. First and Second Church, founded by a congregation in 1630, had many incarnations and survived an almost consuming fire in 1968. The rupture between the old building (1867) and new (1971) was left obvious by the renovation architect, Paul Rudolph. Like ancient Japanese ceramics that break and are reassembled so the fissure and repair are apparent—to emphasize the vessel's preciousness—the church was rebuilt with the old stone Berkeley Street side joined to a dominant, sweeping modern section. The new sanctuary is filled with natural light. As First and Second is a Unitarian congregation, these planes and shafts of light are the room's most prominent decor.

When Christian friends and I wanted to worship together, we went to this welcoming sanctuary. Amnesty International's spring fund-raising concerts were there, and the church was host to many performing arts groups. Across the street, the French Library on Marlborough Street also radiates memories. I saw many a French movie in its paneled rooms, attended friends' weddings (brides descend a curved, carved staircase), and joined in Bastille Day celebrations when Marlborough Street between Berkeley and Clarendon was blocked off for music (Haitian musicians on resonant steel drums), dining, and dancing.

The Charles River was just two blocks from my home on the Avenue, looking much as it does in the nineteenth-century Childe Hassam painting with a gentleman in a top hat musing at the riverbank. Along the river, I had intermittent Edward Goreyesque visions of hospital attendants hurling pans of limbs out the window, this image superimposed on the tranquil, lyric scene, along with poignant memories of the long, conversational walks I had taken with Julie, and the bracing solitary four-mile jogs I took at Thanksgiving when my apartment was filled with inebriated company and the slow-roasting, buttered tea-towel-draped components of the feast. My mental landscape of the river also contained pointy-faced opossums, which I twice saw fast asleep at high noon, dangling like sacks from cherry trees. These pink-blossomed trees with coppery trunks were a gift from the people of Japan to the people of Boston. Limbs (human and botanical), opossums, in-laws, turkeys, cherry blossoms, failed friendship, love across barriers, the good work of Dr. Paul Dudley White and his bicycle paths, and the landscaping traditions of Japan. The path along the Charles River is a crowded walkway for me.

\*   \*   \*

From the start I felt at home in Boston. I grew up in New York and New Hampshire. Boston was not only geographically and geologically in the middle, but was in between in size and society, ecology and appearance. Compared with New York, there are few skyscrapers here, but like New York, Boston is an old port city with 350 years of multiethnic European history, handsome nineteenth-century factory buildings, wharves, and piers; and academic, medical, religious, mercantile, and cultural institutions. People-wise, I found Italians, Latinos, and Irish; African Americans, Asians, and Jews—the same ethnicities, races, and religions I had grown up with in Queens, New York—along with the taciturn but respectful Yankees I knew from New Hampshire. And as in New Hampshire and upstate New York, a Native American presence lingered in Massachusetts: Agawam, Mashpee, Mattapoisett; Scusset Beach, Nauset Marsh; and in Boston, everything from Shawmut Avenue to the Algonquin Club.

Not far from the city, there were mountains, beaches with dunes, and everywhere—still, in 1965!—I could detect the so-called Yankee virtues (privacy, modesty, thrift) I had been raised with, though not a Yankee. Boston's and Cambridge's street trees—little-leaf lindens, Norway maples, pin oaks, ginkgoes, and the grand London plane trees along Cambridge's Memorial Drive (huge trunks with splotchy bark)—were the same as those in New York's five boroughs. In forests and woods were many of my beloved New Hampshire trees: maples, oaks, American beeches (the golden, oval leaves stayed attached during winter); white pines, balsams, hemlocks, and spruce. Boston even had the birds of my combined childhood places: robins, sparrows, cardinals; seagulls, mallards, geese; the eerie, endearing calls of owls at night. And in summer in the evening I would hear a bird I called Night Bird. My boyfriend, with whom I lived on Commonwealth Avenue, and I thought of it as our bird, and assumed there was only one. Years later I learned that it was the common nighthawk, a small, charming creature (most wonderfully, a member of the nightjar family) that feeds on flying insects.

Life here didn't feel as noisy, or crowded, or cutthroat as it did in New York. Boston was small and cohesive. I could walk from the downtown to Brookline. There were parks, trees, and redbrick townhouses, which looked like illustrations from Victorian children's books. I had never seen such houses. I knew the brick bungalows and faux Tudors of Queens, and the farmhouses, wood-frame colonials, and Greek Revivals of northern New Hampshire. Perhaps I had seen a few brownstones in Greenwich Village, but not block upon block of them, kingdoms of tawny stone and red brick along Commonwealth Avenue and Marlborough Street (magnolia trees on the sunny side, dogwoods on the shady), and grouped around the English-style squares of the South End. Generally no more than four or five stories high, they were elegant, tidy, and modest in scale, never overwhelming like the sprawling houses of suburban Long Island.

I didn't learn to drive until I was almost thirty, as a brief experiment in living in the country was coming to an end. There was, and is, no need to drive in Boston, a civilization of neighborhoods. I explored my new city on foot, and using buses, subways, and streetcars. The streetcar or trolley was like something in a French animated film. When the conveyance became unhinged, the trolley-car driver would jump out and quickly, unceremoniously reconnect the overhead wires. Sparks flew, dispersed, and disappeared. The trolley shuddered and returned to life.

Over years of living in Boston neighborhoods, especially the Back Bay, I came to feel that living long portions of our lives in a great city, in a place rich in history, architecture, and human endeavor, can impart meaning and dignity to our efforts, and soothe the small but continual humiliations that come to every life. In a city such as Boston, we see examples of perseverance, accomplishment, and inspiration in the buildings—in our libraries, churches, hospitals, schools. Through all our seasons of failure, foolishness, and blunted hopes, there is, in the community of the great city, the balm of respectable association and the consolation of beauty.

\* \* \*

For all my adult life, I wanted a house of my own, and hoped I would find such a thing in Boston. For decades, I saved. I didn't travel or buy much of anything. I lived on homemade soup, homemade bread, red wine, and coffee. I used the public library, didn't buy records, tapes, or CDs. In winter, unless I had company, I kept my apartments cold. Finally, in 2001, for eleven months, I trawled Greater Boston for a house. I searched in Jamaica Plain, Roslindale, West Roxbury; Cambridge, Somerville, Watertown; East Boston, Arlington, Medford. I found, to my horror and disappointment, scores of decrepit, one-hundred-year-old wood-frame houses with sagging porches, pre–World War II kitchens and baths, and furnaces the size of small rooms, which cost half a million dollars and more. When I had seen over 250 houses, mostly on my own, scouting daily in geographic clusters—leaving my apartment with a thermos, a list, directions, and street maps—I gave up.

Although a city girl, I yielded to the economics of contemporary Boston, and in the winter of 2002 moved a half-hour north where I could afford the quiet, privacy, and space of a 113-year-old Victorian house. The house is gray with white trim, and slowly responding to my care and hard work—my new abilities with cordless drills, cordless hedge trimmers, loppers, pliers, pruners, and prodigious use of joint compound. I would like to say I am a well-adjusted human being, capable of integration, change, and growth. The truth is, I am at present a city girl in exile, an urban woman living in a colony, without a movie theater, museum, bookstore, bagels, crusty bread, concert hall, wine store, ethnic market, ethnic restaurant, pottery studio, girls' gym, and stationery store.

But it is impossible to be ungrateful and unbeguiled by the countryish street where I have found myself, where Genevieve, my ten-year-old neighbor, two houses down, brought me a handmade welcome card mounted on green construction paper, and a packet of marigold seeds, the bleak and lonely winter week I moved in. The two little boys next door show me the insects they have captured in jars for study ("We let them go while they're living," says Ryan, the older brother, age eight). I feed Henry, my neighbors' yellow-lab puppy, miniscule Milkbone puppy biscuits and occasional Stella D'oro margherites, the cookie of my childhood in Queens.

Four or five days each week I travel into Boston, a journey that is both soothing and weird, like having a rendezvous with a former lover. I walk in my old neighborhoods. From the Public Garden down Commonwealth Avenue to the Fenway. From Brookline to Allston to Cambridge. From Audubon Circle to the Riverway to Jamaica Pond. From the Museum of Fine Arts to Mission Hill to Dudley Square, or along Washington Street—from Chinatown to the South End and onward toward Jamaica Plain. From South Station along Atlantic Avenue curling around to the North End. To Haymarket, inland to King's Chapel, Old Boston City Hall, Filene's Basement, Bromfield Pen, and Stoddard's, the oldest store in Boston, where you can buy binoculars, carving knives, and corkscrews.

I had been thinking of these long constitutionals as a fitness routine, but recently I had tea with a pal in New York, and as we talked and ate pumpkin scones, my astute friend asked, "Are you reconstituting yourself?" On the way home, I realized that the long forays I have been taking all over Boston—the treks, schleps, and walkathons—were indeed not so much constitutionals as attempts to reconstitute, to unite the fragments of my experience. I thought I had been dragging myself about familiar streets and neighborhoods like a dray horse, or an old trained bear, when actually, no thanks to my conscious mind, I had been doing higher-order reasoning: the work of integration.

I have loved living in Boston, have loved while living in Boston, and had my heart broken several times (three times in one neighborhood; it must have been the apartment). When I return to the city, the harbor light still shimmers and the Charles River gets choppy in the winter winds. Mallards and gulls bob through the swells. The brownstones of the Back Bay glow as the sun sinks behind them. The vase-shaped zelkova trees along Commonwealth Avenue, planted to replace the diseased, felled elms (I watched the zelkova saplings being dug in and staked decades ago), turn orange, apricot, and gold in autumn. I buy biscotti in the North End, wedges of sweet-potato pie in Dudley Square, and simit, an Armenian breakfast cookie, in Watertown. I ride the trolley car to Brookline, take the bus to Jamaica Plain. I visit the Buddhas at the Museum of Fine Arts, and the rose garden in the Fens, and pause on the arched pedestrian bridge.

I go home. I curl up on my almost-thirty-year-old sofa, in a peaceful, high-ceilinged room. From a distance, I consider my old neighborhoods, and how they overlap, intersect, and connect. I sift through the layers and allow them to fall into place.

# There Goes the Neighborhood

*Michael Patrick MacDonald*

Not long ago, whites wouldn't even drive through Roxbury. For at least two decades following Boston's busing violence, my relatives would devise long, convoluted ways to get from one end of Boston to the other without passing through the most convenient crosstown streets of the city's black neighborhoods. And of course, blacks—and outsiders of any complexion—wouldn't drive through my own Irish neighborhood of South Boston. Now, sitting on a Dudley bus years later, passing the vibrant sights and sounds of a neighborhood alive with kids, street games, arguments, and thumping music, I wondered once again at the similarities between Roxbury and the old Southie. Just then I overheard a conversation that also sounded familiar: about longtime residents having to move out.

Two women in their mid-forties were talking about how their neighborhood was slipping from under their feet. One of the women was in a first-time-home-buyers class, but saw no way she could ever afford to buy in the neighborhood where she'd spent her whole life— *her* neighborhood.

"You hear about that big house up on Dudley Street, the one that used to have all them cousins and the grandma living in it?"

"Uh-uh," the home-buying woman said, leaning back with a scowl of pessimism, sure of the news that was coming. "White people?" she asked knowingly, before her friend could tell her.

"Mm-hm."

They both looked down and shook their heads in what seemed like an all too familiar defeat, before looking across the aisle at me and straightening up together in a posture of defiance.

Do they think that I'm that type of white person? I wondered. After all, how could I be? I come from the projects.

I was glad they would see me stay on the bus beyond Roxbury, proof that I wasn't taking over. Then, after they got off and we began to approach my neighborhood, my own resentment kicked in, as more and more Southie-bound yuppies boarded the bus.

Who are these people taking over our neighborhoods? On the street corners of Boston's balkanized neighborhoods, from "white" Southie to "black" Roxbury, similar suspicions can be heard about *them,* but with different ideas of just who they are, perspectives wrought by the city's historic resentments and divisions of race and class. In Roxbury they might call them "white people," but in Charlestown—once another notorious Irish American enclave of projects, vinyl, and brownstones—the townies call them "toonies," for their resemblance to cartoon characters. "Just goofy looking, ya know?" a townie once explained to me. And at one time, in the early days of 1980s gentrification, before "yuppie" was popularized, kids in both Southie and Charlestown just called them "liberals."

Nationwide, from the Chicano neighborhoods of California to the multiethnic tapestries of Brooklyn, young, often progressive professionals are killing community. And ironically, in Southie these same white newcomers are edging out the racial diversity of an old Irish enclave that had recently started to see hopeful working-class integration. Now Roxbury is becoming hot property, and many people who toiled for years to build community in that neighborhood will have to leave.

But there's really no way to fight gentrification. It always happens overnight. All it takes is for just one of *them* to move in, and, well... there goes the neighborhood.

*   *   *

While realtors trumpet another gritty neighborhood on the rise, and note "improvements in the quality of life" for traditionally working-class South Boston, anyone who *was* woven into the tight-knit community knows that the fabric is in fact being frayed beyond recognition. Long a neighborhood of renters, many are now being forced to move to the suburban hinterlands, unable to compete with the often childless professional's means. Our mostly conservative leadership in Southie had forever distracted the residents from their own economic realities, with warnings of the dire social disaster that blacks would bring to our traditional family (read "white") town. This despite the fact that every one knew the neighborhood code of silence—maintained by homegrown drug lord and FBI-protected informant Whitey Bulger—concealed our own violence, a booming drug trade, and suicides of every kind. Recently, though, after Bulger went on the lam, Southie's long held secrets began to come out, inspired by a budding truth-telling movement of parents and teens.

At the same time, the neighborhood's three large housing projects, long a bastion of poor white resentment of the "other," reached a healthy diversity, one reflective of the city's population: about 50 percent white, 50 percent of color. But before the town was able to totally untie the noose of its isolationism and its long suppressed secrets, Southie itself began to be sold off to developers and speculators as "Boston's best kept secret." It is ironic that this should happen right at the time when we might have seen the birth of a functional, healthy (and even diverse) working-class community.

The old neighborhood sure did have its problems, as would any neighborhood that contained three contiguous census tracts with the highest concentration of white poverty in America, according to a *U.S. News and World Report* study in 1994. But as usual, too many of the best qualities of the old neighborhood will be tossed out with the vinyl siding and exchanged for good taste, permit parking only, anonymity, and streets silenced forever by that upwardly mobile individualism of my cosmopolitan peers.

In Southie I started to hear the beginning of the end with the early morning racket of hammers and saws taken to houses that hadn't been renovated in decades. New people had been buying up and gutting property in what was fast becoming the trendy Boston neighborhood of the 1990s. Some neighborhood people in coffee shops talked about their property values going up, while others talked about becoming homeless with the new high rents. On one particularly noisy morning I decided to try one of the new espresso shops that had opened up. I waited in line with the "outsiders," resentful of their proud talk about "bringing the neighborhood up."

Bobby Got-a-Quarter—a longtime neighborhood fixture—wandered in looking like he'd just woken up, head wobbling, his hand held out for the collection, eyes fixated on the breasts of a female newcomer. He didn't mean anything by it; he just wanted a quarter. The preppy young woman fidgeted nervously, trying not to look at Bobby. Bobby didn't say anything. He's been asking for quarters for so long he doesn't have to ask anymore. You just give him a quarter, those are the rules.

The uneasiness was broken when a Southie guy stepped out of line and poured some coins into Bobby's hand. "No quarters today, Bob, there's five dimes—you can change 'em in for two quarters if ya want." I felt proud then to be one of the people in line who was from the old Southie, with its loyalty and caring for poor souls like Bobby Got-a-Quarter. The Southie girl behind the counter shook two quarters out of her tip cup and slapped them both onto the counter, proud to abide by a neighborhood obligation to Bobby. "Here ya go, Bob, that's for me and Sheila," she said, pointing behind her to the other girl making coffee. Bobby never said anything, not even thank you. He didn't have to. This is Southie, and for better or worse some things are understood in the silence.

Of course, most people moving into urban neighborhoods do so with an excitement for the stories they too will be able to tell, of characters galore and exotic working-class customs, unspoken rules (like the use of kitchen chairs and appliances to save one's parking space—

for the whole winter—after shoveling the car out). Many move into our neighborhoods with a desire for community that they never knew in their middle-class suburban neighborhoods, and cannot find on the Internet, or even in a book club. But gentrification roots out those very qualities, nurtured and mastered over time by people *from* places like Southie or Roxbury. The things that make living in close quarters so appealing: like loyalty, shared struggle and support, the coffee lady knowing your first name (or even calling you "hon" when she doesn't), neighborhood kids ruling the streets with fun, and, moreover, a sense of being connected to something palpable. When one is actually part of such a neighborhood, even the stories at dinner parties or on front stoops feel better. They are not just stories, they are our shared experience, and our connection to a truly American culture.

\*   \*   \*

Perhaps no place epitomizes the American neighborhood as much as Brooklyn, New York. In fact, when Hollywood depicts "blue collar" and "neighborhood," it usually gives it a Brooklyn accent, even if the character is living in the Midwest. From literary classics like *A Tree Grows in Brooklyn* to movies like *Saturday Night Fever* to, more recently, Haitian American hip-hop star Wyclef Jean, Brooklyn, and by definition the American neighborhood, is a part of our cultural landscape.

I was thrilled to move there this year, after two years of working in Los Angeles. For me, the geographic and social landscape of Los Angeles had given me an uneasy sense that felt more like limbo: neither here nor there. After two years of strip malls, people-less sidewalks, and overheard conversations about Mariah Carey's emotional upheavals, I was ready to go home, not only to the East Coast, but to the archetypal American neighborhood: Brooklyn, New York.

Settling into the area west of the Olmsted-designed Prospect Park, I was elated to once again walk streets that shift and change in color, sound, and smell, block by block, minute to minute. To hear people calling up to windows. To see overdressed teenage boys and girls, divided into camps by gender and exchanging mean flirtations with each other. To smell everything from the fresh scali bread being baked behind long-standing bakery walls to New York City trash cooking in the late August heat. And from my first day back—most unlike Los Angeles—I got to actually interact with people, strangers with whom I was somehow connected, from Poland, Italy, the Dominican Republic, Puerto Rico, Ireland, Jamaica, Haiti, and Brooklyn. I felt alive again.

It took a couple of weeks of settling in before I began to notice the impending homogenization of Park Slope and its surrounding areas. Living in what is called Gowanus, at the lower end of the slope, I would walk upslope to Prospect Park, first passing the bodegas and car repair shops of Fourth Avenue; then arriving at Fifth, I'd spot the occasional minimalist-designed restaurant. A cobbler's tiny storefront with a handwritten sign, "Joes Shoes" and the tag line: "Got a shoe problem? Call Joe!" stood right next to a French café that looked like it was shipped piece by piece from Paris, red and yellow rattan chairs, elegantly tiled floors and all. I wondered how long Joe the cobbler would last, and whether I had any shoes he might fix. Maybe the neighborhood would sustain him; I mean, sometimes you need *magret de canard,* but sometimes you need a new sole.

A couple of blocks further up, on Seventh Avenue, I saw the gentrification process complete: more restaurants either right out of Paris or right out of *The Matrix*; lots of blonde babies being wheeled by Jamaican women who provide just about the only diversity on Seventh Avenue these days; and side streets of completely silent Brownstones with no curtains, showcasing the lifestyles of the rich and liberal of Park Slope. I walked the two blocks remaining to get to the unspoiled Prospect Park, but couldn't help fantasizing about living with such high tin ceilings, huge bookshelves, and commanding views of the Slope. Walking back downslope, though, toward life again, I figured it wouldn't be worth it.

I was proud to be living among real folks, but I was really just in the in-between section, an artists' frontier straddling bourgeois convenience and urban realness: trendy gym next to a busy donut shop whose decrepit sign says DEE EE DONU S, the occasional nouveau restaurant, an old vinyl record shop where I scour the bins for Sam

Cooke or vintage Jamaican rock steady, artsy bars next to old-school Puerto Rican or Irish watering holes. Right now there is a really nice mix of ethnicities, lifestyles, and ages in the area at the lower end of the slope.

But I had to start to wonder, how long is it going to last? Am I just pushing the frontiers of yuppie gentrification? I'd never really imagined that someone who'd spent most of his life in a housing project might be part of a gentrifying force. Besides a near lifetime of poverty under my belt, I pride myself on being an activist, whether engaged in specific community organizing efforts in Boston or writing stories. Most of the newcomers to this part of Brooklyn are, like me, artists, with noncorporate jobs. Most artists, like me, gripe about "yuppie invasions" as if we are not part of the process. But really, unlike most of the eleven siblings I grew up with—three of whom died young from the crime and violence of South Boston's streets—I now have enough social capital, enough connections among connected people, and enough income, to rent in a variety of places (save for the avenues closer to Prospect Park!). Landlords can charge me more than they can get from the woman who is feeding three kids on today's non-living-minimum-wage salary. And to live in a place like this, with everything one could dream of in a neighborhood, I have agreed to pay what I can afford. Perhaps in doing so, I'm contributing to the erosion of all that is appealing about this community, just like all those yuppies I've been irked by in Boston.

Artists, too, are gentrifiers. And so are many activists, even if they do not make a lot of money. And yuppies, just like the working poor, can come in all complexions. Sometimes they are Republicans; sometimes they are Democrats. The bankers and traders, the suits who have taken over Manhattan, might be the more conservative types, or, worse, libertarian. But we already know that conservatives and libertarians put the American village, and its children, at a low priority. In places like Boston and much of Brooklyn, though, many of this colonizing class—my class now—would be liberal, and most of us would not even consider ourselves among the vanguard of culture vultures, pushing the frontier that threatens working-class families and the classic American neighborhood. The difference is, we should know better than conservatives. Hopefully many of us do.

\*   \*   \*

On one of the year's first autumn mornings, when the golden light was hitting Brooklyn's rows of brick and vinyl at an altogether new slant, casting clearly demarcated shadows, I walked upslope to the Seventh Avenue Barnes and Noble. I had to do a talk in Manhattan using my book *All Souls*, and had no copy. There is always something weird about buying your own book; you want to tell the cashier, but then again you don't. Will it get you a discount, maybe even good placement in the store? Or will it get you an unimpressed scowl from a twenty-something retro punk hipster? My cashier turned out to be a fifty-something "local lady," with a Southie-type vibe. Lois—that's what her name tag said—exclaimed, "Oh I love this book!" as she swiped the bar code. I told her I wrote it, thinking I might get a discount after all, but also hoping I might get a "welcome to the neighborhood."

"You're kiddin'! You wrote that?" she said, holding up the book and comparing my face to the faces of my siblings on the book jacket. Once she agreed that I looked like the kids on the cover, she called Mary Jo over. Mary Jo seemed to have read the book, too, and that's when the two life-long Park Slope residents opened up to me and went on a lively tirade against yuppies.

"These streets used to be filled with kids!" Mary Jo said, pointing to the now quiet side streets of 1.5-million-dollar homes.

"Everyone knew everyone!" added Lois. It seemed to me that, because I'd written about the similar qualities of Southie and the current demise of the neighborhood, they were more than willing to let me in on their Park Slope resentments. Mary Jo shared her outrage about "play dates" in particular.

"When my kids were growing up they went outside and made friends. Play dates? Oh, these are some sick puppies," she said under her breath, as if we were surrounded by them, and we were.

Then Mary Jo told me something that I wouldn't have believed if Lois hadn't corroborated it. "You should hear the way they talk to us. Ain't that right, Lois?" She told me that the yuppie customers treat her like shit and say, "Who are you? You're no one. Just a cashier." Lois confirmed with a furtive nod, and added that one lady told her that she was just white trash. They both were telling me about having to move because they couldn't afford the community they'd helped to create years ago. Then Mary Jo scooted away and Lois rushed me along with my purchase when they noticed the line behind me, and the panicky approach of a manager, who looked young enough to be their granddaughter.

Walking back downslope, to the area where *I* was the yuppie, I couldn't stop replaying in my head what they'd told me about how they are treated, as an inferior breed. White trash? Now, it wouldn't be inconceivable to me for one person from the working class to merely imagine this type of offense from the more secure classes, but I don't think that two people could invent such a thing. I had to believe their assertions. But even if it weren't true, the fact that such perceptions were being uttered at all didn't bode well for my new neighborhood of Brooklyn, nor, by extension, for the American neighborhood. On my way further downslope, past the burgeoning trendiness of Fifth Avenue, I spotted a *New York Times* headline displayed in a window of a boutique, exclaiming, "Racing Upscale at Full Throttle." The article was announcing that the Fifth Avenue section of Park Slope had "arrived." The lifestyles writer admitted that the lower slope did have its ethnic charm, but that compared to Seventh Avenue, his adopted neighborhood on Fifth had for too long been "a dingy affair."

\* \* \*

Has the neighborhood arrived? Or is it departing? I guess it depends on whom you talk to. Of course there are things we can do and should do, especially those of us who choose to live among the long-achieved connectedness of the urban neighborhood. The choice in particular to reap the benefits of urban diversity (of ethnicity, culture, and class) demands a responsibility to that diversity, nothing less than an activist's vigilance and active community-building work.

The first order of the day is to simply connect. Too often, young professionals, especially those who grew up in more secure and serene settings, are a bit nervous in the neighborhood and therefore do not engage, whether that means holding open a door, saying thank you, or just making eye contact. Besides common decency, everyone who lives in an urban neighborhood should know their neighbors, for everyone's safety. Of course some people prefer the anonymous lifestyle, coming and going from work, socializing in controlled ways. For them there is Manhattan or downtown Boston.

Most of us can afford at least an hour a week to volunteer. Mentoring to promote the social mobility of a neighborhood's children, or fighting for equal access for all kids to the best public education, is what truly improves the quality of life in our cities.

There is currently, too, in most cities a growing affordable-housing movement, most often spurred on by the Industrial Areas Foundation, a grassroots-organizing training movement started by Saul Alinsky. In Brooklyn, community residents have worked miracles in the East New York Brownsville section. In Boston, the IAF affiliate, Greater Boston Interfaith Organization, a faith-based movement across race and class boundaries, has had tremendous success in lobbying for affordable-housing legislation as well as securing millions of dollars to build new affordable-housing units. The mayor of Boston, Thomas Menino, must also be commended for his recent fight to bring rent stabilization to Boston, a citywide grassroots tenant effort that has been repeatedly sabotaged by big real estate interests that have hoodwinked city councilors to vote against the interests of the average working family. Mayor Menino has expressed his concern that Boston is becoming a city of the very rich and the very poor. These efforts, across the country, are all incredibly easy to connect to, and can be searched out on the Internet or at any local library.

Finally, the most important thing we can do right now is work across race and class lines to encourage voter registration, and—through the ballot and through organized community actions—hold all of our elected officials and candidates accountable, at all levels of government. New affordable housing must be built. All families and children in our neighborhoods deserve equal access to the middle class through the best education and job opportunities. If we promote voter registration in our neighborhood, and work to hold our leaders accountable, we will win. And if we truly can work across race and class, reinforcing the qualities that have been perfected in the American neighborhood—things like loyalty, shared struggle and support, the coffee lady knowing your first name (or calling you "hon" when she doesn't), neighborhood kids ruling the streets with fun, and, moreover, a sense of being connected to something palpable—then we will have truly arrived.

# Whose City, Whose Hill?
## The Tradition of Exclusivity
## in Boston Politics

### *Jack Beatty*

The statement "Thomas M. Menino will not inspire a bestselling novel" is as veridical as "The sun will rise in the east." Although Mr. Menino, in 2004 in his third term as mayor of Boston, has served ably, he does not register on the "colorful" scale set by the politicians who have furnished their lives to such novels, Huey Long, the model for "Boss" Willie Stark in Robert Penn Warren's *All the King's Men,* and Boston's James Michael Curley, the scandalous paternity of Frank Skeffington, the aging Irish American mayor in Edwin O'Connor's *The Last Hurrah.* Truly, Boston is the luckier for Menino's pale competence. It takes a whole lot of graft to make a little color. Applied to the likes of Long and Curley, the epithet amounts to verbal slumming. You wouldn't thus garnish a boodler in your city or state, living large on your dollar. "Colorful" lessens the larcenies of other people's pols, or the safely dead.

Over a fifty-year career as ward boss, common councilor, alderman, state representative, four-time congressman and mayor, and one-term governor of Massachusetts, James Michael Curley, twice jailed, many times investigated, lived in a house built by graft, slept between the silk sheets of graft, strode across the Persian carpets of graft, made the grand tour in graft, repaired to the beaches of graft winter and summer, drove in graft's limousines, wore graft's Chesterfield overcoats, ate graft's lobster dinners, smoked graft's cigars, drank graft's whiskey, and left its gratuities—dropping $100 tips during the Depression. "Don't ask me to explain it," he instructed his youngest son, "but never open a checking account."

Curley's last hurrah came in 1951, seeking reelection following a term interrupted by a five-month stay in federal prison for mail fraud—tantamount to Al Capone's being sent to Cicero for tax evasion. "Well, they gave us spaghetti for breakfast . . . and for lunch . . . and at night for dinner," Curley told a reporter who'd asked about the prison menu. "You'd think," he added, "I was a goddamned guinea." He lost the election—and to the city clerk.

If Boston were a vaudeville show it could not have packed in more "color" than the dark-haired, dark-eyed, broad-bellied Curley gave it. Trained by eight years of evening courses at Staley School of the Spoken Word, Curley's voice, a baritone purl, could not perhaps "call in the hogs from the next county"; that distinction belonged to Alben Barkley, the Kentucky senator and Harry Truman's vice president. But what Ben Jonson said of Francis Bacon could be said of Curley (or "Cuh-lee," as he pronounced it): "The fear of every man that heard him was lest he should make an end." This was the "eddie-fying" Curley who left school to support his family after the death of his father, yet quoted Shakespeare copiously in his speeches and to lacquer his peculations in grandeur—at least once or twice a term Curley would find himself "naked to mine enemies." That cultured chap shared the same self as the brawler who slugged a hostile editor at high noon on Devonshire Street. "Did you see the mayor slap him down?" a messenger boy who witnessed the fight asked a reporter. "It was just one bang and then curtains."

If his fists furnished spots of color, his dirty tricks were good for rainbows. "He deliberately cheapens himself in a campaign," a sympathetic columnist observed. Choosing examples is like picking the most heartbreaking Red Sox team ever.

Curley's "poison-gas squad" would mix with crowds and loudly inventory the perfidies of his opponents. "Have you heard that John R. Murphy was seen eating meat last Friday at the Copley Plaza?" "No! But, say, what can you expect of the thirty-three-degree Mason?" Curley had young supporters knock on doors at midnight in Irish South Boston, pretending to be members of a Baptist Church club canvassing for the other guy. He planted hecklers who knew how to take a punch, which he'd deliver like Tom Mix. Running for governor in 1924 Curley barnstormed across Massachusetts, and wherever he spoke, it seemed, crosses burned on distant hills. Pointing to the blasphemous blazes, Curley issued defiances. "If any Klansmen wish to meet us on the dark and lonely road," he told a crowd in Athol, "they are welcome to make the attempt." At the time, the fortuitous conjunction of man and prop aroused suspicions. ("There are four million people in Massachusetts and the only one who has ever found a burning cross is James M. Curley," as one Republican legislator marveled.) In his autobiography Curley came clean: The "Klansmen" were his boys.

Exposing sexual peccadilloes ranked as his signature dirty trick. He won his first term as mayor, in 1913, by threatening to make public, in a course of lectures entitled "Great Lovers in History: From Cleopatra to Toodles," the incumbent mayor's dalliance with a cigarette girl, Elizabeth "Toodles" Ryan, the same age as his daughter Rose, the future mother of John F. Kennedy. Under pressure from his daughter and wife, John F. Fitzgerald withdrew from the race. As mayor, Curley blackmailed three Paramount Pictures executives, all married, who had inadvisably participated in what one newspaper called "a midnight frolic" at a roadhouse within rumor-range of His Honor. The frolic earned its name when a giant silver salver was put before the moguls, the cover lifted off, and a pulchritudinous woman stepped out wearing "a few pieces of parsley and a sprinkling of salad dressing."

Above all, in your daily newspaper sure as the funny pages, Curley made you laugh. Of a wealthy car-dealer running against him for governor, he remarked, "[The people] will not send a gilded nonentity to Beacon Hill." "If we have another era of Hoover," he quipped,

"Gandhi will be the best-dressed man in America!" He ascribed the collapse of an off-ramp built by one of his pet contractors to "an injudicious mixture of sand and cement." When a man not known to be among his supporters congratulated him on his greatest triumph, adding, "I think you'll be a great governor," Curley replied, "Very nice of you to say that, Bill. Do say it behind my back some day."

A fabulous fifty-year act. But by 1951 Boston's economy was a basket case owing in punishing part to Curley's business-killing, bribe-producing taxes on commercial real estate. So Bostonians retired the old stager to the House of Graft at 350 The Jamaicaway, the brick mansion with the shamrock shutters.

*   *   *

Curley occupies an emblematic place in Boston's 370-plus-year argument over the question "Whose city and whose hill?" Down the centuries, Puritans, Yankees, and Irish alike answered, "Ours." Exclusivity passed from one to another and hung on like a bad cold. "Why should I travel," the apocryphal Beacon Hill lady remarked for the ages, "when I'm already here." Here was swell if you belonged to the dominant group, but the out-groups—including Quakers, Irish Catholics, Jews, and African Americans—got the back of Boston's hand. Born to Irish immigrant parents in 1874, James Michael Curley entered a city changing owners. He rose on a green tide.

Post–Civil War Boston still belonged to a Yankee Protestant ascendancy that stretched back to the late seventeenth century, the last time the city changed hands. "The city upon a hill" of John Winthrop's Puritan theocracy meant their city and their hill. No Quakers or non-Congregationalist Protestants need apply. Apply? Boston's Taliban hung the Quaker Mary Dyer on Boston Common. They banished Anne Hutchinson for teaching that personal revelation could supplant biblical authority. She wound up in the Dutch settlement at Pelham Bay, in the Bronx, where she and her fourteen children were killed in an Indian attack. The Puritans drove Roger Williams into the darkness of Rhode Island. And any "papist" who trespassed into the Bay Colony never made that mistake again. Ann Glover, accused of being a secret Catholic, was hanged as a witch in 1688; and as late as 1700 the legislature passed a ban on Catholic priests. "The design of our first planters," John Cotton later wrote of the founders of the Bay Colony, "was not toleration . . . [they] were professed enemies of it. . . . Their business was to settle . . . and secure Religion to Posterity according to the way in which they believed in God."

As Boston grew into the chief fishery and port of the colonies, Puritan success threatened Puritan virtue. Noting with satisfaction that "this town is the Very Mart of the Land, French, Portugalls and Dutch come hither for Traffique," a Puritan commentator also feared a falling away: "Whereas he hath purposely pickt out this People for a patterne of purity and soundnesse of Doctrine, as well as Discipline, that all such may find a refuge among you, and let not any Merchants, Innkeepers, Taverners and men of Trade in hope of gaine, fling open the gates so wide, as that by letting in all sorts you mar the worke of Christ intended." Boston could no longer afford such qualms. Responding to merchants' protests that intolerance "makes us stinke everywhere," the General Court made property, not faith, the criterion of voting, ensuring that killjoys in the councils of government would ask, "Yes, roasting Catholics on the Common would be grand, but wouldn't it be bad for business?"

Boston entered the eighteenth century as a merchant's town, led by an aristocracy of trade. The Olivers, Fanueils, Wentworths, Bowdoins, and Apthrops married one another, locking up their daughters before risers like the Hancocks could get at them. Entering the nineteenth century, fortune-fledged by the China, India, and slave trades, the merchant families of the revolutionary era consummated what Samuel Eliot Morison called "the marriage of wharf and waterfall," launching the industrial revolution in America at a mill along the Charles River in Waltham and then at an industrial city they constructed on farmland along the Merrimack River and named for one of their own—Lowell. In his novel *Elsie Venner,* Oliver Wendell Holmes called them the "Boston Brahmins," with "their houses by Bulfinch, their monopoly of Beacon Street, their ancestral portraits and Chinese porcelains, humanitarianism, Unitarian faith in the march of the mind, Yankee shrewdness, and New England exclusiveness." Through the first half of the century, Boston was their city and Beacon their hill, a light unto all the nations but one.

\* \* \*

The Irish Famine of the late 1840s remains the controlling political fact in Boston's post-Revolutionary history. The Irish differed from later immigrants in degree of desperation. Hunger, as much as hope, drove them to America. Eighty and more years after the Famine, Irish-American fathers, before saying grace at supper, would declare to the bewilderment of the youngest child, "So long as there's meat on the shin of a sparrow, we'll eat in this house." Taking that in, the child would wonder at looking for meat there, and fear would take a grip on his mind.

For the year 1840 fewer than 4,000 Irish arrived in Boston. On one April day in 1847, more than 1,000 debarked. By 1850 the Irish numbered 35,000 in a population of 136,900. They lived in cellars and "rookeries" along the Boston waterfront, breeding smallpox, cholera, tuberculosis, and children, who were, in the words of a census taker, "literally born to die." Poor relief tripled in six years. Groggeries—twelve hundred by 1849—proliferated. Drunkenness brought crime; between 1843 and 1848 "attempts to kill," as the Boston Police Court called assault by pistol, knife, club, bottle, fist, and foot, went up by an unacceptable 1,700 percent. Unacceptable in the most cultured city in America—in 1848 Boston published 120 periodicals with a total circulation of over half a million. Unacceptable to Beacon Hill ladies so proper that they blacked out the erotic lines in Byron and Shelley and were now afraid to walk across the Common. Profoundly unacceptable to Protestant working men, watching the desperate Irish bid their wages down. Summing up the changes wrought by the Irish in the "once orderly city of the Pilgrims," one Yankee observer judged that they were "about equivalent to a social revolution." Revolutions beget counterrevolutions, and in the 1850s Protestant Massachusetts struck back.

A secret society that limited its members to persons "born of Protestant parents, reared under Protestant influence, and not united in marriage with a Roman Catholic," formed in secret lodges across the Commonwealth, linked by passwords and handshakes and identified as the "Know-Nothings" after the members' response to queries about its purpose—"I know nothing about it"—surfaced in the elections of 1854. By an historic margin, they elected one of their own as mayor of Boston and installed Know-Nothings in all the state's constitutional offices, including governor, and in 379 of the 381 seats in the Massachusetts legislature. The society's purpose now became clear: to use state power to persecute the Irish. The Know-Nothings passed a constitutional amendment forbidding Catholics from holding state jobs, disbanded Boston's Irish militia, made the King James Bible required reading in the public schools, and, under a "pauper removal law," swept up more than thirteen hundred Irish paupers from the state's almshouses and shipped them to Liverpool. That the Know-Nothings styled themselves "reformers"—champions of compulsory education, vaccination for children, women's rights, and abolition—made "reform" a dirty word to the Boston Irish. Those opponents he did not defame as Episcopalian converts (the Irish lampooned "God's frozen people"), Curley cudgeled as "reformers," mainlining a prejudice etched in the Irish political unconscious by the Know-Nothing pogrom.

History quickly overtook the Know-Nothings as anti-slavery, trumping anti-immigration, subsumed northern politics. By the presidential election of 1856, they had been absorbed into a new party, the anti-slavery Republicans, who inherited a century of immigrant enmity as the price of the Know-Nothing infusion. The 1850s set down the enduring grammar of Massachusetts politics: The Irish were Democrats, the native Yankee Protestants Republicans. In 1860 Stephen A. Douglas, the Democratic presidential nominee, drew a crowd of ten thousand to an October rally in Irish Fort Hill. A month later, Boston's two Irish wards went heavily for Douglas while Abraham Lincoln carried every other ward in the city overwhelmingly. This cleavage, solidified by class and neighborhood segregation, proved enduring. A representative scion of the Boston Irish, I was twenty-one when I met my first Protestant, who efficiently doubled as my first Republican.

Sundered Boston became one in the Civil War. A fighting people and proud of it, the Irish were at last wanted by the Yankee community. The Irish opposed abolition, fearing the competition for work and wages of three million freedmen. But the crisis of the Union overrode their aversion to what the Catholic *Pilot* called "Niggerology." If before the attack on Fort Sumter the abolitionists had talked sedition, the southern secessionists had now lit the blaze of rebellion itself. For this generation of Irish, with its immigrant's reverence for established authority, that put the South irrevocably in the wrong. "We Catholics have only one course," the *Pilot* editorialized, "stand by the Union, fight for the Union, die by the Union."

When, shortly after Sumter fell, a ship from Savannah flying the Confederate flag docked in Boston, a largely Irish mob demanded that the captain not only run down his colors but surrender them. He did, and the Irish tore the flag to pieces and bore the remnants through the streets of the North End. They raised a regiment and Governor John Andrew presented it with a green silk flag inscribed "Thy Sons by Adoption; Thy firm Supporters and Defenders from Duty, Affection, and Choice." (In the Hall of Flags at the State House, that green flag was closest to the catafalque holding James Curley's body as one hundred thousand mourners filed past through the day and night of November 12, 1958.) In the Ninth Massachusetts, and in Meagher's Irish Brigade, at Malvern Hill, Fredericksburg, Gettysburg, and Spotsylvania Courthouse, names that once stiffened men's spines, the Irish died their way into Yankee Boston's wary esteem.

"The Puritan has passed; the Catholic remains," William Henry Cardinal O'Connell declared in a 1910 speech marking the centenary of the Boston archdiocese. Although less memorable as language, O'Connell's words are the equal, in historical weight, to John Winthrop's "City on a Hill" address. "The city," O'Connell continued, "where a century ago he came unwanted he has made his own. The child of the immigrant is called in to fill the place which the Puritan has left." O'Connell's predecessor, Archbishop John J. Williams, had refused the Cardinal's red hat—it might provoke the Protestants. "We want no aggressive Catholics in Boston," he said. But O'Connell spoke for a people whose numbers had finally told their power. "It is time," he wrote in 1915, "for Catholic manhood to stand erect, square its shoulders, look the world in the eye and say, 'I am a Roman Catholic citizen; What about it?'"

The Irish surge in politics fed from the fire of O'Connell's Church Triumphant. Boston elected its first Irish Catholic mayor, Hugh

O'Brien, in 1883 and its last Yankee Protestant, Malcolm Nichols, in 1925, and then only because Jim Curley, prevented from succeeding himself by a state law (passed to accomplish just that) swung the election to Nichols by cluttering the ballot with Irish names.

Reviewing the autobiography of Charles Francis Adams, Cardinal O'Connell adumbrated a staple of Curley's politics of polarization, observing, "The wonder is psychological and physiological that there were ever any children at all in the Puritan home." For decades, Curley, the father of seven children, would exploit this taunting theme—the frigidity of the Protestant bed next to the carnival of sexuality held annually in the Catholic. To Curley sex was politics by other means; the carnal act made Democrats.

The year before O'Connell's adieu to the Puritan, Curley played the sex card in attacking the editor of the *Boston Traveler,* a man who had called Curley's election to the board of aldermen "an insult to the city"—because Curley had been elected while in jail for taking a postal exam for a constituent who, Curley said, "could not spell Constantinople but had the feet for a mailman." The Republican paper's motto, "Fit for the Home," Curley charged, ill comported with some of its advertisements. "A clean sheet, fit to go into the home?" Curley asked in a speech before his colleagues on the board. "I refer Mr. McSweeney [the editor] to page No. 3, the bottom of the first column, and ask him if he feels that that is a fit ad, to take into the home of a decent family—the illuminated ad of an article intended to destroy life, to prevent children coming into the world?" The ad—for the "wonderful Marvel Whirling Spray...the best-safest-most convenient, it cleans instantly...new vaginal syringe"—depicted a contraceptive appliance modeled on the bellows of a Bessemer furnace. Contraception would mean "the race suicide" of the Irish. Why, look what it had done to the Protestant vote!

Only Curley could make a leash law the occasion for ethnic mischief over bulldogs, squirrels, and children. The Committee on Public Improvements had decreed that all dogs in Boston should be leashed "except dogs on Boston Common." Curley wanted the phrase struck from the ordinance. "I recognize that the product of Ward 10 [the Back Bay] should have some place to recreate, and since they do not produce children in large numbers in Ward 10, and do produce bulldogs, it might perhaps be proper to permit them to recreate on the Common. But the Common is a place of recreation for squirrels that . . . were there in large numbers some years ago, and of late years have almost been wiped out because of the existence of the bulldogs. The squirrel is a very beautiful animal. It compares very favorably with the bull dog . . . and while perhaps it is not as lovable as a household pet in Ward 10 as the natural product of Ward 10 — bulldogs — it still affords amusement and considerable pleasure to the children who occasionally are permitted to pass through the Common." Curley never missed a chance to remind the worthies of Back Bay and Beacon Hill that they were the remnant of a vanished supremacy.

Curley spoke with patronizing affection of the "newer races" — Jews, Italians, Syrians, Greeks, Poles — who had arrived in Boston in the early twentieth century. But in politics, in the civil service, in the schools, in the police and fire departments, "on" the Edison, the phone company, the gas company, and the transit authority, the Irish ruled for fifty years.

They gave ground slowly and sometimes, as during the Boston busing crisis of the 1970s, bitterly. Like whites in other cities across the country in the postwar era, the Irish moved out of the city, some to escape a growing black population, others to fulfill a dream of lawns. They migrated to the South Shore, as the Yankees before them, fleeing their Irish ancestors, had to the North, their politics changing with their address. By the 1980s, in the ultimate sign of assimilation, many of the children and grandchildren of the Irish Democracy of Fitzgerald, Curley, Al Smith, John F. Kennedy, and Tip O'Neill had absconded, God bless the mark, to the Republican Party. America, it has been said, is the euthanasia of memories.

\* \* \*

My Boston friends include émigrés from Iowa, Colorado, New Jersey, New York, and Illinois. The flags of Caribbean countries — of Haiti, Jamaica, Antigua, Grenada, and Trinidad and Tobago — hang in St. Matthew's, my old parish church, in Dorchester. Dorchester Avenue, which runs past St. Margaret's, St. William's, St. Ambrose's, St. Mark's, and St. Gregory's, in places looks like a Vietnamese boulevard. St. Peter's, where I received my first Communion, has Vietnamese priests. Along Brighton Avenue, in Allston, the ecumenical palate has its pick of Russian, Korean, Greek, Middle Eastern, and Thai cuisines. "Allston-Brighton Free Radio," Thomas H. O'Connor, the dean of Boston historians, writes in *The Hub: Boston Past and Present,* "includes programs in Spanish, Portuguese, Ethiopian, and Eritrean music." Newcomers to Boston have bid up the value of real estate in two fading Irish neighborhoods, Charlestown and South Boston. My aunt, who washed dishes at South Boston High School for forty-four years and raised a beautiful blond daughter in her apartment on West Broadway, would have trouble paying the rent there today. The South End, Skid Row forty years ago, ranks as Boston's chicest neighborhood, a magnet for young sophisticates, as once for winos. Curley's Jamaica Plain is a Hispanic stronghold. And what would "Himself" make of Boston's newest nursery—the Back Bay, where you take your life in your hands dodging the carriages and trikes? Squirrels gambol on the Common, toddlers, not bulldogs, chasing.

Today Boston is a minority majority city, meaning no one group can claim it as *their* city. The Puritan has passed, and the Brahmin, and the green tide recedes farther every year. No election of the twenty-first century will feature a shamrock roster like the mayoral preliminary of 1983: Flynn, Kiely, Finnegan, Kearney, and (how did he get in there?) DiCara. The November final, pitting South Boston's Raymond Flynn against Boston's first African-American mayoral candidate, former state representative Mel King, ended one era and began another. Flynn won but, a hundred years after Hugh O'Brien became the first, he may turn out to have been Boston's last Irish American mayor. Tom Menino (whose father, born in Grottamindara in Avellino, worked for thirty-five years at the Westinghouse plant in Hyde Park that now houses a multicultural public high school, the Academy of the Pacific Rim) inaugurated a tradition of future firsts when he became Boston's first Italian-American mayor, in 1993.

High-rise glass and aluminum-skinned towers block the landward view that John Winthrop enjoyed from the deck of the *Arbella,* obscuring what's left of the hill he must have been elated was *there,* the symbolic topography anticipated by his metaphor. "We must," he charged his community weeks before the *Arbella* sailed into the harbor, "bear one and other's burdens. . . . We must be willing to abridge ourselves of our superfluities for the supply of other's necessities. For we must consider that we shall be as a City upon a Hill. The eyes of all people are upon us." It was as if he already saw Boston in his mind's eye with a hope uncontaminated by history, a vision still on the waves, seeking a land.

# Isabella Stewart Gardner's Museum: A Legacy for America

*Alan Chong*

Just over a hundred years ago, on January 1, 1903, Isabella Stewart Gardner (1840–1924) opened her museum, then called Fenway Court, for the first time. The tall, plain building stood entirely alone in the Fenway, a newly reclaimed district along a park designed by Frederick Law Olmsted on the edge of Boston. Enthroned like some Renaissance monarch, she greeted her guests on a raised dais. Members of the Boston Symphony Orchestra then performed a short concert in the small auditorium, at the conclusion of which, mirrored doors were rolled back to reveal a glass-roofed courtyard. With walls stained a delicate pink, the space was filled with lush flowers and plants arranged among ancient columns and statuary. Guests wandered into the court and up into galleries laden with paintings, sculpture, textiles, and furniture. Although it was well known that Isabella Gardner had been collecting important paintings by Titian, Rembrandt, van Dyck, Rubens, and Fra Angelico since the mid-1890s, the full extent and variety of the collection was unsuspected, while the installation of the objects was entirely surprising.

Contemporary praise of the individual objects in the collection was always combined with appreciation of Isabella's personal role in the concept of the museum and of her philanthropy. Charles Eliot Norton wrote in 1902: "Palace and gallery (there is no other word for it) are such an exhibition of the genius of a woman of wealth as never seen before. The building, of which she is the sole architect, is admirably designed. I know of no private collection in Europe which compares with this in the uniform level of the works it contains." Henry James similarly celebrated "the unaided and quite heroic genius of a private citizen." For James, the Gardner Museum felt simultaneously private and public—and this remains the essence of the museum's power. Indeed, since I arrived at the Gardner Museum as curator in 1999, I have found that many visitors assume the museum is simply Isabella Gardner's private residence now opened to visitors, as is the case with many noble collections and country houses in Europe. However, the structure was expressly designed and built as a public museum, and specifically organized for its long-term preservation. Thus, while the arrangement of the collection is personal and atmospheric, the institution is in many ways a thoroughly modern construct.

Isabella Gardner had long played an influential role in Boston's cultural scene, initially as a keen supporter of the Boston Symphony Orchestra and the Boston Public Library, and even as an organizer of small concerts in her Beacon Street home. In the 1890s, she considered buying James McNeill Whistler's celebrated Peacock Room (now in the Freer Gallery of Art, Washington) for the new library, and she supported the commissions granted John Singer Sargent and Joseph Lindon Smith. Much of her collection seems to have been earmarked for the Museum of Fine Arts in Boston (where her husband, Jack Gardner, was a trustee and treasurer), until she decided to create her own institution. Even after the opening of Fenway Court in 1903, the fate of the two museums remained intertwined. The newly reclaimed Fenway neighborhood was intended as Boston's cultural district: Symphony Hall (which opened in 1902) provided the gateway to institutions like the Harvard Medical School (1906), the Museum of Fine Arts (1909), and the Gardner Museum (1903). Mrs. Gardner was first on the block, and a few months after she broke ground, the Museum of Fine Arts purchased land for its new building, which would be considerably larger than its old home on Copley Square. Isabella Gardner was greatly interested in museum administration, and became close friends with trustees, curators, and administrators—to the extent that her influence was sometimes resented by those who disagreed with her. She was especially close to Okakura Kakuzo and Matthew Prichard, Asian curator and assistant director, respectively, of the Museum of Fine Arts. Isabella was drawn into an internal dispute at that museum over the display of plaster casts with works of art; she argued forcefully that the originals must be the principal feature of any museum, and forced the ouster of the director, Edward Robinson, who nonetheless later became director of the Metropolitan Museum of Art. In addition, the Fogg Museum at Harvard University had been founded in 1895 to provide a collection of casts, reproductions, and other study materials for the use of students. Close to many of the founders of the Fogg, Isabella Gardner seems to have consciously designed her museum to be as different from the Fogg as possible—not only to display original works of great beauty, but also to present such objects in an atmospheric environment, rather than in a scholarly or "analytical" manner.

Several distinctive features of Isabella's patronage of the arts have proven influential with respect to American arts philanthropy. Before the Isabella Stewart Gardner Museum was established, a few attempts had been made to open private museums in the United States, and some private collections had been absorbed into public collections. In the 1860s, for example, Thomas Jefferson Bryant and James Jackson Jarves tried to set up museums in New York based on their collections of old master paintings, but with only limited success. Bryant's paintings were incorporated into the New York Historical Society, which has regrettably sold his paintings over the last few decades; Jarves's notable collection of early Italian paintings was sold to Yale College and absorbed into its art gallery.

Isabella Gardner was entirely different in the attention and control she lavished on every aspect of her museum: She constructed a building to exacting standards, purchased architectural elements for its decoration, and arranged the galleries herself. After Fenway Court opened, she continued to add to the collection and rethink its display. In 1915 an entire wing of the building was rebuilt in order to provide new settings for some of her objects, namely a collection of tapestries and John Singer Sargent's expansive homage to the excitement and passion of flamenco, *El Jaleo*. Most crucially, she provided for her museum's future. Here, as in so many of her gestures, Isabella's actions had both positive and negative repercussions. The museum was to be governed by an independent board of trustees whose principal responsibility was to appoint the future directors of the museum (she had ensured that her own choice, Morris Carter, could not be removed). She also placed several strictures on the conduct of the trustees, including a famous injunction that they not alter the general disposition of art in the galleries. In a very modern way, these restrictions did not apply to the professional director, who was given wide discretion in the museum's operation; it seems that Mrs. Gardner was anticipating the interfering ways of many American museum trustees, who were often businessmen accustomed to wielding authority, but not authorities on art, although they sometimes had strong opinions about running institutions.

Gardner also left her new museum with a generous endowment for its operation, something most previous personal museums had lacked. She scrimped and saved for the last ten years of her life to ensure that she would leave at least a million dollars. This frugality, combined with the austerity of World War I and a debilitating stroke she suffered in 1919, made for a spare existence at the museum. She wanted to make a few last acquisitions for Fenway Court, but found Italian Renaissance paintings mostly out of her reach, so instead began to acquire Spanish painting and sculpture, as well as examples of Islamic and Asian art. Most painful for her, she could not purchase *The Feast of the Gods* by Titian and Bellini (now in the National Gallery of Art, Washington); she nearly had sufficient funds, but did not want to dip into endowment capital. Her parsimony guaranteed the financial health of the museum.

An inheritor of considerable wealth, Isabella Gardner was conscious of her privileged position in American society, as well as an obligation to do something in return. Her will and the charter of her museum explicitly mandated a museum trust "for the education and enjoyment of the public forever." This, together with provisions for the independent governance and financial security of the museum, became a model for later museums. In 1917 she expanded on her intents in a letter to someone who had tried to buy some of the works of art at Fenway Court:

> Years ago, I decided that the great need in our Country was Art. We were large developing the other sides. We were a young country and had very few opportunities of seeing beautiful things, works of art etc. So I determined to make it my life work if I could. Therefore, ever since my parents died I spent every cent I inherited (for that was my money) in bringing about the object of my life. So, you see for my personal needs I cannot possibly sell any work of art. I economize as much as possible with the income of Mr. Gardner's money left to me. The principal I shall never touch. I economize with the income because what I save goes to the upkeep of my ideal project.

Moreover, it was a modern professional museum, despite its quaint and (to some) eccentric appearance and layout. The endowment and professional director furthered museum scholarship: A scholarly catalogue of the paintings was published in 1932, and the second director, George Stout, had trained as a painting conservator and was a pioneer in U.S. conservation practice. These were important legacies for the small museum in America.

The 1890s was the age of the "house museum" in Europe, as a handful of opulent private residences, filled with splendid treasures, were being opened to the public. The Museo Poldi Pezzoli in Milan was formed by Gian Giacomo Poldi-Pezzoli between the 1840s and 1870s. Isabella Gardner had visited it as a girl, and it was reported that the evocatively displayed treasures sparked her desire to create a similar museum if she ever had the means. The Musée Jacquemart-André in Paris was formed by a couple, Édouard André and Nélie Jacquemart, in the 1880s and 1890s; their passionate interest in Italian painting and sculpture may also have inspired Mrs. Gardner. The museum was not opened until 1912, although this was long anticipated, and unusually, it came with an endowment of 5 million francs. In London, the Wallace Collection had largely been formed by the fourth marquess of Hertford in Paris around 1850. It was left to the British nation and opened in 1900. When Jack and Isabella Gardner first decided to build a museum for the public around 1897 (the deed of incorporation was drawn up in 1899), there was no real model for an independent private museum—especially one not owned by a government body. The Musée Jacquemart-André and the Wallace Collection were not yet open, and none of these institutions came with the financial resources to guarantee their independence.

In its turn, the Gardner Museum also opened new possibilities on the American cultural landscape. Private collectors, especially of eclectic and unusual material, could now believe that there was historical and aesthetic value to intimate settings, personal display techniques, and intriguing juxtapositions of objects. In many ways, the museum founded in New York by Henry Clay Frick was an outgrowth of Mrs. Gardner's grand project. A robber baron and monopolist, Frick possessed far greater wealth than Gardner. They shared interests in painters like Bellini, Titian, and Whistler, but otherwise their tastes were quite different. Frick also bought the vast majority of his paintings after 1901, by which time Gardner had already made her greatest acquisitions. What they shared was the singularity of vision for a personal museum, and the foresightedness to endow their institutions. It was at first rumored that Frick would build a gallery at his summer home in Prides Crossing, Massachusetts, bringing his museum into direct competition with Fenway Court; Frick bragged to the *New York Times* that both his collection and his building would exceed those of Gardner's. In the end he turned his back on Massachusetts and his hometown, Pittsburgh, in favor of New York. Frick's deed of incorporation directly echoed Gardner's in creating a museum "for the use and benefit of all persons whomsoever." What is not immediately apparent to today's visitor to the Frick Collection is the extent of changes made to it since Frick's day. He died in 1919 and his widow lived in the building until 1933, after which much of the gallery was rebuilt and reconfigured. Rooms on the second floor destined for small-scale galleries were turned into offices. On the other hand, no major alterations have been made to Mrs. Gardner's galleries since her death in 1924, and the display and combinations of objects continue to mirror her intimate approach to art.

After the opening of the Gardner Museum, a new type of museum took hold in America: The Cloisters in New York, the Walters Art Gallery (now renamed the Walters Art Museum) in Baltimore, the Phillips Collection in Washington, and the Huntington Library in Pasadena have preserved essential aspects of their founders' intents, even as they expanded and metamorphosed. The Freer Gallery of Art in Washington and the Taft Museum in Cincinnati retain more completely the atmosphere of the original installation. In more recent years, the personal and eclectic visions of the Menil Foundation in Houston and the Wolfsonian Museum in Miami Beach are especially praiseworthy.

There are also certain less desirable traits that have their origin with the Isabella Stewart Gardner Museum and the other private museums born in that era. While it might seem logical—in our own age of donor recognition, where naming rights to just about anything can be bought—that a collector would give her name to an institution of her own fashioning, this was not a given in the nineteenth century. In fact, Isabella Gardner first intended to call the museum Fenway Court, and it was called that until 1924 when it was revealed not only that the museum was legally incorporated as the Isabella Stewart Gardner Museum but that a stone plaque with that title had been secretly installed on the building's facade. During her lifetime, Mrs. Gardner had even written to local publishers asking them to refrain from using the term "Gardner Museum," insisting on "Fenway Court." Museums were named in various ways: The Wallace Collection does not bear the name of its founding collector, the Marquess of Hertford. Museums could also be memorials, as in the case of the Leland Stanford Jr. Museum, founded in 1894 (recently renamed the Cantor Center for Visual Arts). The desire for commemoration and personal control could have its downside as well. For example, three of the four founders of the Los Angeles County Museum—J. Paul Getty, Armand Hammer, and Norton Simon—deserted that institution to form their own personal museums. The Barnes Foundation outside Philadelphia shares many features with the Gardner Museum, in particular the collecting abilities of its founders. Albert Barnes also possessed a strong sense of his museum's future direction, and he developed a philosophy of art to perpetuate this vision—an approach that can be illuminating as well as restrictive.

For all of the charm of the Gardner Museum and the striking personality of Isabella herself, we would pay little attention to the institution without its collection of significant works of art, distinctively varied and carefully chosen. Before her, few Americans had attempted to form a balanced collection of Renaissance paintings and decorative arts; Gardner also pursued classical and medieval sculpture, manuscripts and drawings, and the work of living artists. With taste and considerable luck, Isabella Gardner started off by securing a rare painting by Johannes Vermeer at a Paris auction in 1892. She soon realized that she needed expert guidance, and she turned to Charles Eliot Norton and then Bernard Berenson for advice, while also relying on other friends to discover treasures for her. Berenson is often singled out as the authority behind the Gardner collection, and to be sure he helped Isabella buy crucial paintings like Titian's *Europa* and works by Botticelli, Fra Angelico, Rembrandt, and Rubens. At the same time, Isabella herself firmly decided the direction her collection would take: She turned away from early interests in English and Dutch paintings to focus primarily on the Italian Renaissance. Moreover, the furniture and textiles appear to have been exclusively of her own selection.

Bernard Berenson's exact role was complex. When he began advising Gardner in 1894, he was young and virtually unknown as an art expert; indeed, she seems to have wanted to help him by employing him occasionally as a consultant. By the end of the century, however, he was widely celebrated as the consultant who had enabled Gardner to amass a truly astounding collection of pictures in a very short period of time. She bought famous paintings, often at record high prices, and here the story becomes more complicated, for documents now reveal that Berenson was closely tied to a London dealer, Colnaghi's, and its director Otto Gutekunst. Their correspondence and account books reveal that nearly every object Berenson "discovered" for Gardner was owned or represented by Colnaghi, although Berenson often claimed to have found the paintings in forgotten estates and dusty palaces. Further, he and Colnaghi were taking large profits from their sales to Gardner. None of this was illegal or even unethical, but Mrs. Gardner was deeply distrustful of dealers, Colnaghi's in particular, and knew nothing of this special arrangement. Gardner normally paid Berenson a 5 percent commission plus expenses, and Berenson went through great pains to disguise the source of her paintings and the percentage of his profits from her purchases.

The subterfuge began to unravel in 1898 because other dealers jealous of the cozy and lucrative arrangement began to leak details about the real prices of Mrs. Gardner's paintings. Her husband, Jack, became incensed and threatened to sue Colnaghi's and Berenson, who became despondent, almost suicidal (according to his wife, Mary). What really worried Berenson was the threat to his reputation, since he was now on his way to becoming one of the world's great connoisseurs. He risked exposure as a mere salesman who greedily took percentages from all sides. Otto Gutekunst had to reassure Berenson: "You must not worry and fret like a nervous young woman. Surely the money you and we have made all along was *easily* made." Gutekunst then suggested that in the future it might be safer to be honest with Mrs. Gardner, and simply add 10 or 15 percent to the original prices. This never happened, and the crisis between Gardner and Berenson soon passed, in part because of the death of Jack Gardner in December 1898. Isabella continued to make purchases from Berenson.

Isabella Gardner's money had been made by her parents and her husband's parents, principally during the 1860s, through diverse investments in mining, railways, and steel in the Midwest. Isabella and Jack's fortune, a little less than $5 million in 1895, while substantial, would not have placed them among the richest Americans. And they certainly could not be reckoned in the same company as the new industrial tycoons—the robber barons: Rockefeller from Cleveland; Carnegie, Mellon, and Frick from Pittsburgh; Widener in Philadelphia; or Morgan in New York. Around 1900, Frick, Widener, and Morgan (the "squillionaires," according to Isabella) also began to collect old master paintings, sending that market spiraling upward. This now drove the best Italian paintings beyond the reach of Mrs. Gardner, who wrote "with tears streaming down my cheeks, because I haven't Morgan's money" and (in 1907): "Woe is me! Why am I not Morgan or Frick?"

No greater contrast between collectors existed than that between Isabella Gardner and J. P. Morgan. Where Isabella carefully selected individual objects, Morgan amassed great quantities of art, often buying up entire collections: the library of William Bennett of Manchester, James Garland's vast array of Chinese porcelain, and the Hoentschel collection of medieval sculpture and decorative arts. Gardner had spent approximately $2.5 million on her collection; Morgan more than $20 million.

Contemporary critics often compared Morgan's approach to collecting with Mrs. Gardner's, a contrast evident when most of Morgan's collection was displayed in the Metropolitan Museum of Art in 1914. The *New Republic* compared Gardner's judicious acquisitions and loving display with the whole-scale acquisitiveness of Morgan: "This practice of unending accumulation, which displays everything and reveals nothing, is the direct result of a policy of mere acquisition, seemingly the only policy our museums are able to conceive. The modern collector hoards what he usually has neither the time to see nor the space to house.... Imagine, instead of these well-ordered salesrooms, an apse built into a wall, an altar beneath a stained glass window, the reliquaries, the lamps and the bishop's crook in their destined places, tapestries hiding the walls." These were the very strategies favored by Gardner, as well as by later collectors like George Gray Barnard, the founder of the Cloisters in New York.

Isabella Stewart Gardner faced innumerable barriers to achieving her dream. Taste and wealth were not enough to create a museum: Energy and drive were also required, which she had in abundance. She was, perhaps, less fortunate in the field of politics, something other American collectors of her era like Frick and Morgan intuitively understood, given their business experience. Gardner faced considerable resistance from the federal and municipal governments, in part because a philanthropic enterprise like the Gardner Museum had never really been attempted before. In 1897 the federal government imposed a 20 percent duty on imported works of art. Exempted from this "luxury tax" were works of art to be exhibited for educational purposes, and Gardner assumed that her considerable purchases abroad were in the clear since the museum was constituted as a charitable trust. However, the Treasury Department ruled against her because Fenway Court was open to the public for only a few weeks a year, as would be the case until 1925. She was thus forced to pay a whopping $200,000 on the million dollars' worth of art she had imported. She faced another grave crisis in 1908. After many years of tough negotiations with the help of the painter Joseph Lindon Smith, she had acquired Piero della Francesco's fresco depicting Hercules. Since she was so famous as an art collector, Isabella asked a friend, Emily Crane Chadbourne (who was also an art collector) to bring the painting into America for her by shipping it through Canada to Chicago. Moreover, the value was falsely declared as $5,000, rather than the actual $82,000. The customs office seized the shipment and released it only when the duty and fine (totaling the value of the shipment) had been paid. The import duty on antique works of art was soon lifted in 1910, enabling more-cautious collectors like J. P. Morgan to bring their European holdings to America.

Not all observers have found the Gardner museum to their taste, and indeed from its very inception there have been skeptical voices. The decor was vaguely Venetian and a little Asian, whereas most museums built around 1900, like most government edifices of the period, were classically inspired, Beaux-Arts buildings. Massive marble (and decidedly masculine) structures, enriched with columns and arches—as seen, for example, in the Boston Public Library and the new Museum of Fine Arts built just next door to Fenway Court—were anathema to Isabella, who reportedly called them mausoleums. Her narrow, dark blue hallways, eclectically arranged galleries, and cluttered alcoves seemed old-fashioned and Victorian to many. It is no surprise that Edith Wharton, who wrote a book on decorating in the grand French style, was less than overwhelmed by Fenway Court: "Of course have seen Palazzo Gardner. Her collection is marvelous, and looks beautifully in its new setting, but a spirit of opposition roused in me when I am told 'there is nothing like it in Europe' especially when this is applied to houses." Mary Berenson in 1920 wrote that she and her husband, Bernard, found that the Gardner Museum

looks to our now enlightened eyes like a junk shop. There is something horrible in these American collections, in snatching this and that away from its real home and hanging it on a wall of priceless damask made for somewhere else, above furniture higgledpiggled from other places, strewn with objets d'art ravished from still other realms, Chinese, Japanese, Persian, Indian objects, that seem as if they were bleeding to death in those dreary super-museums.

For a modernist critic like Lewis Mumford, the richly atmospheric setting of the Gardner Museum was merely fake Romanticism. He favored clinically white walls and sparse, empty interiors —a different sort of Orientalism. "She seized objects; lugged them to Boston; and enthroned them in a building which was—one hardly knows which to call it—a home and a museum. As a home, it became a pattern for the homes of rich people in America for a whole generation." It is fascinating that Charles Eliot Norton, Henry James, and Lewis Mumford all employ the identical rhetorical device of confusion: Was Fenway Court a home or a gallery—a public space or a private one?

The multiplicity of identities of the Gardner Museum is an almost unique legacy. In Mrs. Gardner's day, Fenway Court was filled not just with beautiful works of art, but also with musical performances, poetry readings, and, at its center, luxuriant flowers. Artists, writers, and thinkers were invited to live and work in the museum. Mrs. Gardner seemed intent on creating a true museum in its original sense: a place where all of the muses—all of the arts—could be experienced. The present-day Gardner Museum strives to honor that legacy with a diversified program, a challenge few art museums can attempt.

The true impact and influence of a collector or an individual patron can sometimes be difficult to fully appreciate in the modern world. The patron is often derided as elitist, interested only in self-aggrandizement. Moreover, an intensely personal vision of art— a characteristic of any good collector—tends to inspire a certain amount of resistance, and a strong personality can seem eccentric, willful, or even narrow-minded to outside observers unless a genuine attempt is made to enter into the spirit of such an individual.

The Gardner Museum (like several other small, personal museums) differs from most modern American museums. In place of bright, bustling galleries presented in didactic and often simplistic fashion, the Gardner Museum unveils its treasures as part of a more complete and atmospheric experience, full of ambiguous half-tints and mysterious shadows. Visitors are free to wander and experience art at their own pace. Isabella Gardner shied away from verbose and analytic art history, preferring more poetic and deliberately vague responses. Her museum asks questions, but does not always provide easy answers. This type of private emotional response is not terribly popular in our precision-driven world, but it may be the most valuable aspect of Isabella Stewart Gardner's legacy in the arts.

# A Splendid Anachronism

## *James Miller*

In the spring of 2002, I was invited to join one of Boston's most charmingly idiosyncratic institutions, a club called the Examiner. On the first Monday night of every month from October through May, members of this club meet to have dinner and hear a talk by one of their colleagues, followed by discussion. This is not the oldest such club in Boston—the Wednesday-evening club was founded in 1777 and included among its first members John Adams. But since 1863, the Examiner has met without interruption—even in the midst of wars. Consisting today of roughly forty members, it has consistently tried to bring together community leaders interested in the enlightenment of society.

Early members included a number of New England luminaries: Ralph Waldo Emerson, the prophet of self-reliance and founder of America's most durable civil religion, the reformation movement that he and his disciples called transcendentalism; Henry James Sr., a theologian and the patriarch of Boston's first and so far only intellectual dynasty, who in 1872 addressed the Examiner club on the topic of "the genius and influence of Emerson"; William James, Henry's firstborn son, who became America's first great psychologist and also helped to stimulate intellectual interest in the philosophical movement known as pragmatism; William Dean Howells, who edited the *Atlantic Monthly* from 1871 until 1881 and helped popularize the fiction of Henry James Jr. and Mark Twain; Charles Eliot Norton, who helped found the *Nation* magazine in 1865 and in later years lectured on the history of art at Harvard University; and Francis Parkman Jr., one of America's preeminent nineteenth-century historians, who dramatized the rivalry between France and England over the conquering of North America.

"Not bad company," remarked my old friend and fellow Examiner, Robert Kuttner, a syndicated columnist and editor of the feistiest of our contemporary liberal journals, the *American Prospect*. Not that I needed convincing, but Bob explained why I should set aside Monday nights and pony up the modest annual dues: Although the setting was stuffy and the food invariably uninspired, he explained, the conversation was usually good.

We discussed the irony of the occasion. Neither of us felt like we were fitting heirs of the intellectual traditions represented by Emerson and James. I certainly lack Emerson's serene confidence in the power of genius to revolutionize the culture of my country. In the late nineteenth century, a gifted Bostonian might seriously entertain such a prospect. But not today. Not in an age when the likes of O. J. Simpson, Monica Lewinsky, and Michael Jackson hold in thrall the collective imagination, even in stodgy old Boston.

Still—and in part precisely because the club seemed like such a splendid anachronism—I eagerly accepted my invitation to join.

My first dinner was followed by remarks by Ellen Hume (a media analyst and former political correspondent for the *Wall Street Journal*). Ellen talked about her experience living in Prague as the wife of the American ambassador to the Czech Republic under the Clinton administration. The other club members talked about the prospects for democracy around the world since the fall of the Soviet Union. It was all very civilized—and a far cry from the three-ring media circus waiting for me when I returned home to my cable television.

Since I am a historian by training, I was curious to find out more about how this club had got its start and how it had managed to survive. And since the Examiner, like any good Boston establishment, is an institution proud of its history, my curiosity was soon gratified. The set of documents sent to every new member included a copy of a talk about the club's founding and early history, delivered in 1978 by longtime Examiner Frank M. Coffin, who served two terms as a U.S. representative from Maine before being appointed to the United States Court of Appeals for the First Circuit in 1965.

"The Examiner was born on May 21, 1863," Coffin explained, "the first meeting being held at the Parker House a week later on May 28. Except for two or three meetings at the Union Club"—the club's current home more than 140 years later—"all meetings were held at the Parker House, beginning at 4 or 5 P.M., followed by what was described as 'New England high tea,' with no ceremony, no 'soup and fish.'"

The club took its name from the *Christian Examiner,* a Unitarian periodical founded in 1824. In the decades that followed, the *Examiner* published a number of important essays by authors like George Ripley and Orestes Brownson, debating the proper understanding of social reform, religious faith, and transcendental idealism, and generally criticizing the Calvinist orthodoxy promoted by such rival periodicals as Lyman Beecher's *Spirit of the Pilgrims.*

But by 1863, the journal had fallen on hard times (it would cease publication six years later, in 1869). In that year, J. H. Allen agreed to establish a partnership to publish the journal, on the condition that a group of former editors called the Examiner Association be dissolved and replaced by a newly constituted club. Its membership would be broadened to include not just clerics, but representatives of all the professions, and with an emphasis on "future efficiency rather than usefulness in the past."

The origin of the club casts an interesting light on its contemporary composition. The Christian link was severed years ago: A considerable proportion of members are Jewish, and I don't think we have a single minister among our membership, Unitarian or otherwise, though the author and columnist James Carroll was a Catholic priest before becoming one of the church's most outspoken liberal critics.

What we do have is a large number of members with experience in the world of journalism from a wide variety of publications, nationally known but Boston based, including the city's liberal daily, the *Boston Globe;* the weekly *New England Journal of Medicine;* the *Atlantic;* and the quarterly *Daedalus,* published by the American Academy of Arts and Sciences, based in Cambridge.

In addition, there are several doctors and judges and businesspeople in the group; and also a large number of professors from the area's universities. It is a distinguished and convivial group, by design, and it is also overwhelmingly liberal in outlook, perhaps because members annually vote on whom to invite to join, and most of these members share certain opinions about what is right and proper in politics and society. A straw poll held one Monday night before the 2002 Massachusetts gubernatorial election revealed that not a single member present that evening was voting for Republican Mitt Romney.

The results of our straw poll almost convinced me that we Examiners were perhaps after all perfectly fitting heirs to Emerson, James, et al. Like our famed precursors, we were on the whole articulate and reasonable souls, as sober and exquisitely moderated in our liberal faith as the mainstream Unitarian ministers who had founded the club in the first place.

And yet there was pathos for me in that moment of recognition. Once attuned to the wilder strains of radicalism that rocked American society in the 1960s, I was reared by a father steeped in the traditions of prairie populism championed by William Jennings Bryan and the International Workers of the World. The cultural traditions behind my own somewhat unruly political convictions left me feeling a little like a barbarian at the gates as I listened to my fellow Examiners deplore in the kindest and gentlest of terms the pending election of a former venture capitalist as governor of my state.

I soon discovered, however, that the club welcomed all views, perhaps to a fault. I present myself as an example: To the evident horror of the club's current president, Douglas P. Woodlock, a judge in the U.S. District Court in Boston, I blithely suggested one evening that we Americans jettison our jury system and opt instead either for civil trials conducted by a panel of expert judges, as under European law, or genuinely democratic trials decided by a large jury of several hundred randomly selected citizens, as was done in ancient Athens.

According to Frank Coffin, such speculative flights of fancy were by no means unusual, even in the club's early history. "In February of 1870," wrote Coffin, "the Club had a go at perennial issues raised by those who contemplate history: Is man diminishing in energy? increasing in size? becoming less moral? more barbaric? This session prompted such remarks as that the ancient Greeks could see farther than Indians, that armor in the Tower of London and Dresden clearly were to be worn by men larger than today's variety, that the retreat of the 10,000 (and 200 women) described by Xenophon would have strained modern man to the utmost, and that 'It is . . . a curious fact that in our late war the Maine backwoodsmen gave out before the city clerks.'"

This litany of foolish remarks, carefully preserved because the club's secretary keeps meticulous minutes of each meeting, is probably a salutary reminder of how silly even the supposed "best and the brightest" can sound when they are winging it among friends.

Generally, though, the remarks of the members are well-informed and our conversations are fairly earnest—though reading Coffin's history of the club, I could not help but wonder if our predecessors didn't perhaps treat the club's conversations far more earnestly still. Boston to this day arguably boasts one of the greatest concentrations of literary and scientific intelligence in the history of the human world—but it has been many decades since anyone has seriously supposed that America's culture radiates out from a hub centered on Beacon Hill (where the Examiner Club in fact meets).

In the spring of 2003, Robert Kuttner addressed the club about the prospects for liberalism in America. That night, he chose to accentuate the positive, not to deny the difficulties that Democrats faced, but to convince us, and perhaps himself, that the cause of liberal reform wasn't hopeless.

It was a cogent and clear call to arms, but I found I had little to say, mainly because I was unconvinced that our views really made much of a difference. The future of American politics, I mused, lay not with writers and scholars and talkers like ourselves, but rather with pollsters and unlettered politicians, entrepreneurs unashamed to sell their souls to the rich, leaders anxious to tell people what they want to hear—in short, political operatives profoundly uninterested in the type of upright liberality of spirit and intellectual self-reliance that we Examiners presumably epitomized.

How different the world must have seemed at the time of the club's founding! In the decades before, Emerson had crisscrossed the United States, giving lectures to eager audiences of ordinary artisans and workers, preaching secular sermons meant to inspire daring and creativity, and to spread his secular gospel of intelligent individualism. In this mission, Emerson was in some ways wildly successful, inspiring the poetry of Walt Whitman and the pragmatism of William James and John Dewey. But in other ways, what really has triumphed in America is not the stern idealism of Emerson, but rather an utterly trivializing version of individualistic uplift, expressed for example in meaningless sound bites like "Be all that you can be"—a recruiting slogan in recent years for the U.S. Army. The earnest struggles of Unitarians and transcendentalists to reform New England's fierce Puritan heritage, and the passionate debates of the pragmatists over the varieties of religious experience and the future of democracy in America, have devolved into the hollow messages of media bent on mass marketing a dizzying variety of individual lifestyles to a growing number of Americans who rely on over-the-counter goods and services to furnish whatever sense of "self" they fancy they need to win friends and influence people.

As a result, the cultural preconditions that once put New England at the cutting edge of defining the American prospect no longer obtain. The information sciences and biotechnology—key areas of global growth in the years to come—form thriving sectors of Boston's intellectual life at the start of a new millennium. But the broadly shared religious assumptions that made what Boston's intellectuals thought seem of moment to the country at large disappeared long ago, weakened by the very success of a trivialized transcendentalism—and then banished altogether by the arrival of successive waves of immigrants raised as Catholics, Jews, Muslims, Hindus, Buddhists, each group animated by its own distinctive beliefs and convictions about the promise of America.

In the last three decades of the nineteenth century, the members of the Examiner Club discoursed on socialism, evolution, the right method of teaching history—and many of their views had a wider resonance in America's politics and culture. In the opening years of the twenty-first century, the members of the club have discoursed on the future of liberalism, the flaws of the jury system, the disgrace of medical care in this country—and few of our views are liable to have currency anytime soon in the broader political culture.

This is not to suggest that I plan to resign my membership in the Examiner Club. It is a great group of people, and I enjoy the companionship—and liberality—of their minds. I also like the sense that we are, in our own modest way, swimming against the tide of history, united by our unfashionable love of talk and ideas.

And that is why the Examiner is one Boston institution that is liable to survive for many years to come. For over our dinner table, something of the original spirit of the transcendentalist reformation lives on. Emerson was right: Conversations like ours, consequential or not, are "a friendly sign of the survival of the love of letters amongst a people too busy to give to letters anymore."

# Boston's Children
# and the Power of Play

*Irene Smalls*

Dawn Smalls and Jonathan Smalls. It is through my own children, and their lilliputian locomotion, that I have come to know Boston as a city of and for children. I say "locomotion" because my children were always on the move, walking, running, and playing, and in Boston they have a good city to play with. In fact, in contemplating Boston as a city for children, I would like to take a serious look at play, for play is the work of children.

From Boston's tiny tot lots to the Fenway Rose Garden to the magnificent green spaces of Olmsted's landscapes, the city of Boston offers its young citizens 273 parks. Added to these formal recreational areas are the countless impromptu play spaces that young people create for themselves. A fine example is the steps of the Boston Public Library, which have recently become a beloved spot for Boston's young skateboarders to perform "ollies" and other gymnastic tricks. Not only Boston's physical spaces, but the city's climate is a factor in play. This city's four distinct seasons take turns in asking for a child's hand in play: In winter, the nearest snowbank offers material for fun; in fall, Boston's children always have bunches of leaves to crunch and jump into; the Swan Boats of the Public Garden are an annual harbinger of warm weather; and as the temperature rises in summer, Italian ices fuel prances through Boston Common. Still later, Boston's Scooper Bowl on City Hall Plaza presents children approximately one zillion flavors of ice cream; this event allowed my daughter Dawn to do extensive research into cherry vanilla, French vanilla, vanilla with caramel swirl, et cetera, all possible variations on her favorite flavor.

Boston is a famously walkable city. Its walkability includes not only the historically significant interpretive walks along the Freedom Trail, Women's Heritage Trail, and Black Heritage Trail, but the countless ordinary sidewalks that invite children and their parents to dally and frisk about and explore the surprises of the urban world. One of my books recounts just such a walk, which my son and I took one day through Boston's South End. *Jonathan and His Mommy* tells the story of how we turned a walk into a memorable promenade, zigzagging, giant-stepping, hip-hopping, crazy-crisscrossing, and reggaeing through the wide streets of the South End. Even Robert McCloskey's classic, *Make Way for Ducklings,* is about a Boston walk, as Mama Mallard and the ducklings Jack, Kack, Lack, Mack, Nack, Ouack, Pack, and Quack make their way around their home ground in the Boston Public Garden.

Dawn and Jonathan and I are now veteran walkers in a city we love, and over the years, we found many special routes that suited our moods and interests. One of the walks we enjoyed most begins at the lovely reflecting pool at the Christian Science Center, a 670-foot-long, 100-foot-wide pool that is located adjacent to a beautiful garden. The pool is a perfect body of water for miniature-sailboat races, and Dawn and Jonathan liked to chatter with the seagulls and swans they discovered wading in the water. In addition, the reflecting pool has 144 spray jets—or sprinklers, as we think of them—which provide a joyful experience for a child (and their mother), a cool spritzing on a hot summer day. After the refreshments of the reflecting pool, we liked to walk the few yards to the Mapparium, a unique space where you can tread lightly over a pure glass bridge into a cavernous riot of color. The Mapparium is a stained-glass globe, 30 feet in diameter and illuminated by hundreds of small lights that electrify the colors. Here is a tip: Whatever else you do in the Mapparium, don't stamp your feet and clap your hands at the same time. As we learned, the sound is deafening; any noise made in the space is multiplied intensely because (science lesson): Glass does not absorb sound.

Leaving the Mapparium, we would wander to Boylston Street and the Boston Public Library. Passing the grand ladies of the Boston Public Library, the allegorical sculptures that represent Science and Art, we would enter through mammoth doors that open into the grand marble lobby and staircase of the McKim Building (the old research library). There, inside the lobby, are the couchant lions, a pair of unpolished marble lions sculpted by Louis St. Gaudens, which inspired the title of the PBS kid's show *Between the Lions*. Continuing south across Boylston Street, we would step onto exclusive Newbury Street and peek into some of the city's art galleries, which are always free to the public. Our next destination was the nearby Boston Public Garden, the oldest botanical garden in the country. In spring, it was our ritual to take a spin on the Swan Boats, which ply the small lagoon in the center of the garden. At only a quarter for a ride, my daughter loved sometimes paying her own way. I confess that a Swan Boat ride is what I imagine heavenly transport must be like: On these silent craft, which are propelled by a captain pedaling bicycle-like gear, you skim the water's surface smoothly, moving at two miles per hour, often followed by a flotilla of ducks, the whole assembly countering the fast pace of the surrounding world. The sun caresses your skin, and you glide past huge weeping willows whose long fronds seem only to add to the coolness of the ride. My daughter had only one complaint about the Swan Boat ride: It was never long enough.

Departing from the Swan Boat dock, we took exactly twelve steps up to a small stone bridge and proceeded from the Public Garden into the adjacent Boston Common. There we always liked to stop and admire the ornate Victorian fountain that features ladies, birds, and a little boy, all spewing water. From Boston Common we walked up from the Public Garden to the point where Winter Street turns into Summer Street, an intersection marked by an enormous sculpture. Officially titled *Helion,* to a child's eye the sculpture appears to be a gargantuan, humongous amalgamation of twenty-six-foot-tall brilliant-orange lollipops.

After this feast for the eyes, we continued on Summer Street until it intersects with Congress Street, where we would spot the landmark of the Children's Museum, a former snack-stand in the shape of an old-fashioned milk bottle. This wooden milk bottle, an artifact of 1940s American roadside life, cleverly reimagined by the Children's Museum, also serves a menu of appealing snacks. Heading toward the museum, we banked left on Congress Street, passing the *Beaver II*, a replica of the seventeenth-century British brig commonly known as the Boston Tea Party ship. The *Beaver II* has ceremonial bales of tea on board for "tossing" into Boston Harbor in honor of that historic tea toss that took place the night of December 16, 1773. At the Children's Museum, located just across the Fort Point Channel from the Tea Party ship, Boston's children find an endless amount of daily, messy fun, songs and stories, the Shimmy-and-Shake program, and brilliant interactive exhibits. The museum also operates a small satellite location at Logan Airport. Located in Terminals A and C, the Kidport features a thingamabob that whizzes, whacks, and whistles, as well as an irresistible baggage-claim slide and a mural of mirrors.

\* \* \*

The Kidport, like many Boston pleasures, is free, and for many families in Boston, including mine, that is important. My children and I learned to love Boston for free, and even a partial list of the city's free things to do with children is impressive: On Fridays, the Children's Museum is free for children under five. There are also free Friday flicks on the Esplanade along the Charles River; many times my children and I enjoyed an hour at the Children's Museum, then headed over to the river to catch the breezes and the picture show. With green grass and the Charles River as a backdrop, the Esplanade Hatch Shell is my hands-down candidate for Boston's best movie and concert venue. Once a year the spectacle of spectacles also occurs there, when the Hatch Shell is the site of Boston's Fourth of July birthday party for America, with the Boston Pops performing and a half million citizens in attendance.

Other free activities in Boston include: ice-skating at the Prudential Center and at the Frog Pond on Boston Common; square-dancing in Copley Square Park; concerts in all the parks; Summer Thing; ski trips organized by the YES Program; tennis lessons at Sparrow Park; the Boston Parks Department's sport leagues; and gospel concerts at the New England Conservatory of Music during Black History Month. The neighborhood branch libraries of the Boston Public Library offer citizens programs as well as free passes to city treasures: the Museum of Fine Arts, the Isabella Stewart Gardner Museum, the Science Museum, the Children's Museum, the Franklin Park Zoo, and the New England Aquarium. The Afro-American Museum on Beacon Hill offers free programs, including historical overnights. Read Boston's bookmobile has free book give-aways. There are free Victorian-house tours, including the Gibson House on Beacon Street and several must-see mansions on Commonwealth Avenue. Also neighborhood house and garden tours, and Open Studios exhibits throughout the city, showcasing the work of local artists.

To this list of generous resources for the children of Boston, I must add one significant caveat. Almost all of the activities, resources, and places my children and I enjoyed are located in Boston proper, not in the outlying neighborhoods. The streets of downtown Boston lead into the city's sixteen distinctive neighborhoods, residential areas that are Boston on a child's scale: smaller, familiar, friend-size places that are home to most of the city's children. It is on the city's neighborhood sidewalks that children count cracks (so as not to break a mother's back), learn to play hopscotch, marbles, and tag, and carry on that enduring jump-rope art form known as double Dutch. Boston is now a minority majority city, and the neighborhoods are rightly admired for their multiplicity of ethnicities. Our city's neighborhoods contain the small shops and neighborhood figures that children come to know and trust as they grow up. The experience of all these more-intimate neighborhood-eye-views of the city are important for children, helping them gain a sense of identity as they become Bostonians retaining the particular ethnic flavor of their own families and communities.

But in spite of the rich intimacy of neighborhood life, there is a critical lack of cultural and recreational resources in the city's neighborhoods. Although our local branch libraries, and to some extent the Parks Department, do a commendable job in providing programs and special events in the neighborhoods, most things free are located downtown. Because my children and I lived near the heart of the city, the shows, concerts, art galleries, and museums we liked were only walking distance away from our front door, but this is not true for the majority of Boston's children. And of course, even if an event or activity is "free," there is always a cost in terms of logistics, the expense of time and money required for transportation from the neighborhoods. In other words, poor children and their families have to pay to go to free activities. For many of them, the costs are formidable.

For Boston to be a good city for children, and for all children, it must really be a good city for families, because 87 percent of Boston's children live in families. Taking a quick look at the makeup of Boston's population today, we see the percentage of children dropping, a loss that is traceable largely to changes in economics and housing and to issues about schools. When I moved to the city in the early 1980s, I moved into midtown Boston, where apartments were inexpensive and easy to find. At that time, St. Botolph Street was a predominately black neighborhood (there were only three white families on my street). It was also an ideal place for families because the housing stock included huge, floor-through three- and four-bedroom apartments. On our block at that time, the street was alive with children playing stickball and ring-a-levio and jumping rope. Within the next ten years, 90 percent of the children were gone, and all of the children above five years old were gone. The racial demographics had inverted too; my family had become one of only three black families living on the street. What was at work, of course, was the economics of gentrification.

Information from the Boston Redevelopment Authority confirms my firsthand experience: Since 1980, Boston's youth population has fallen by 40 percent as families with children have been forced to move farther and farther out of the city because of their inability to pay increasing real estate taxes and rents in the city proper. Most of Boston's young people, almost half, are now concentrated in

Dorchester, Roxbury, and Mattapan, neighborhoods with the most affordable housing stock. And today, my old St. Botolph Street neighborhood is a much different place. The neighborhood is fairly homogeneous; by and large the households have no children, or if they have children there is only one. Once that child turns five years old, his or her family usually packs up and leaves Boston for suburbia and the suburban schools. Simply put, to be a truly good city for children, Boston needs much more affordable housing. Downtown Boston, Back Bay, St. Botolph Street, and Beacon Hill are the neighborhoods with the best transportation, play spaces, amenities, and recreational resources. These four neighborhoods with less than 2 percent of the city's children are where housing is most expensive. Indeed, in some of the wealthier neighborhoods, parents have gotten city land to build and fund their own play spaces and small events. At Easter time in the St. Botolph Street neighborhood, there were pony rides in the local park funded by the friends of Sparrow Park. In making Boston a good city, affordable housing must be created, so that many more children and their families can live in the downtown neighborhoods that provide the most enrichment and stimulation.

\* \* \*

Just who are Boston's children? Here is a quick portrait from the 2000 U.S. Census: Our city has 32,046 children under age five, and 84,513 young people ages five to seventeen, or a total of 116,559 babies, toddlers, young children, preteens, and teenagers. Boston's children are 85 percent minority and 15 percent white. There are 60,626 students (75 percent of Boston's children) attending Boston public schools. Fifty percent of the students in the public schools come from Dorchester and Roxbury. The federal school lunch program services 72 percent of Boston public school students as income-eligible for free or reduced-price lunches. These figures tell us that when we are talking about Boston's children, we are talking mostly about children from lower-middle- to low-income families.

As we think about the children of the city, I propose that we expand our definition of children in one important way. In an article, "The Space of Play," published in the RSA Journal of London's Royal Society for the Arts, the architects Franco La Cecla and Lucy Bullivant describe how children inhabit a world shaped by adults, and how opportunities for play are increasingly limited by a lack of vision in how space is planned. La Cecla and Bullivant also believe that fulfilling the need for children's play brings important benefits to adults as well as to the young. Following their thesis, I would like to extend the definition of "child," and address two constituencies of children. The first constituency is the 20 percent of Boston's population under the age of eighteen. The second constituency is adults, including the children over age eighteen who continue to live at home with their parents. The good city nurtures its young, and also the young at heart, and embraces the importance of fun and play for all ages. We all have heard the old saying "All work and no play makes Jack a dull boy." The modern equivalent of that saying is "All work and no play makes Jack an overweight, stressed-out, depressed, and dull boy." Some adults know intuitively how to stay in touch with their playful natures; others, perhaps especially in a city with Boston's sense of reserve, might need some convincing. Whatever your temperament, consider the many benefits of play.

**Play is vital to good education.** In 2003, an early-education principal in the Boston Public Schools told me that in some Boston kindergartens, nap time and playtime have been curtailed to allow more time for academic instruction. This is counter to established wisdom. In an article in *Educational Leadership* magazine, "Putting Early Academics in Their Place," Marilou Hyson highlights a research project done in the late 1980s which showed very clearly that the most effective early-childhood classrooms offered children play that fostered social and emotional development as well as nurturing their academic skills. Later research described in "The Importance of Being Playful" by Elena Bodrova and Deborah J. Leong (also in *Educational Leadership*), provides an even stronger connection between the quality of play in the preschool years and children's readiness for school instruction. The article states that mature play or open-ended play is most important, and describes such play as characterized by: imaginary situations, multiple roles, clearly defined rules, flexible themes, language development, and sufficient time. This type of play helps to develop students' cognitive skills.

*Play is healthy.* There are 59 million obese adults, according to the Center for Disease Control. Obesity in children has reached epidemic proportions. Statistics from *Prevention* magazine show that there are 9 million overweight children in America. There are many causes, including diet, but a major contributing factor is the lack of play. Kids are eating more high-calorie foods and engaging in less physical activity. Only 25 percent of schools today offer physical education or gym programs. If obese individuals don't slim down by age twenty, their lives are shortened by almost twenty years. Such individuals are also more likely to suffer from diabetes, heart disease, and other weight-related ailments. The American School Health Association has asserted that "during childhood, physical and psychological health are related to participation in regular physical activity or play." Real play, not the passive play of watching television, movies, or playing video games. Exercise guidelines issued by the American Heart Association recommend that children over age two engage in enjoyable physical activity thirty minutes a day, and have thirty minutes or more of more vigorous exercise three to four times a week to maintain heart and lung fitness. According to the association, activity is particularly helpful for the physical and psychological well being of children with weight problems. In some environments, concern for children's safety outdoors has greatly eroded their freedom to play. While passive play is hazardous to health, it is safe in the sense that children are easily monitored and there are no moving parts that could possibly cause injury. But concerns about safety should not be preventing us from teaching our children to lead healthful lives.

Psychologists say that children laugh about one hundred times a day, while the average adult laughs twice a day. Adults need to laugh more. The importance of the giggle factor is vastly underestimated. As author Judith Stones writes in *Health,* "Laugh and your whole cardiovascular system laughs with you." There is a laundry list of reasons why laughter is great for us. "Laughing helps expand the capillaries increasing blood and oxygen throughout your body" says Michael Miller, M.D., director of the Center for Preventive Cardiology at the University of Maryland's Medical Center in Baltimore. Those expanded capillaries help prevent heart attacks and stroke. Research has demonstrated that laughter also relieves stress and prolongs life; reduces blood sugar levels; boosts our immune system and other defenses against infections; and lowers blood levels of hormones associated with stress.

* * *

Boston is an old city with a definite sense of itself, but for all its history Boston is still brand-new when seen with the eyes of a child. This is a city that offers, simultaneously, qualities of a small town and virtues of an international, world-class city. But of course, like all cities, Boston has challenges. Perhaps our greatest challenge now is to create the affordable housing that will allow low- and lower-middle-income families with children to makes their homes and lives in the city. In addition, Boston's major cultural institutions should be encouraged to locate in the neighborhoods and provide more programming there. Boston City Hall needs to make a concerted effort to have special activities happen all over the city so that the poor don't have to pay more for access. And for the health of Boston, I hope that we can increase the amount and quality of play in this city. We can begin in our public schools. One innovative approach to increasing academic performance and the health of all children is to creatively incorporate literature as well as math concepts into our children's play spaces.

Our Parks Department also warrants our attention; now that budgets have been cut, we must think creatively about ways to maintain and expand the quality of urban green space, which has been shown to contribute positively to health, social inclusion, sustainability, and urban renewal. And although children can and do play anywhere, studies point to the importance of green space as a particularly adaptive locale for open-ended play, the kind of play in which children can make their own decisions and explore their own thought processes.

Beyond the parks and the schools, Boston, and cities everywhere, can do much to design buildings and public spaces with laughter and play in mind, knowing that such locations are vital to the well-being of both children and adults. Indeed, the good city has places and things in it that are there just to make us laugh, spots of wonder and pure fun. Urban developers must be asked, as a normal part of their plans, to provide amusing places, green places, play spaces for children, and things to see and experience that can make us smile on an office plaza, in a park, or in the midst of a courthouse. It would be good for business, and good for the business of living.

Children exist at that fabulous intersection of heart, mind, and body where play emerges spontaneously and creatively. Adults are also an integration of mind, body, and spirit, and still have that capacity for play that releases us from sterile and stressful lives. My wish for this city is that we will create more places of whimsy and wow, that we proper Bostonians loosen up a little and laugh a lot. Let us play!

# Good Sports, Bad Sports

*Howard Bryant*

By Friday, less than twenty-four hours after the fall—by which I mean, of course, the fall of the 2003 Red Sox—a sharp, bitter wind swept lariat-like through the Muddy Creek basin in the Fenway section of town where the Red Sox play. If you weren't a member of the initiated, the weather signaled only the regular arrival of another season, albeit a storied one. But for the diehard baseball fans of Boston, the piercing gusts were not simply a low-pressure system moving in from the west, but a force of empathy—nature expressing her sympathy for the loss to the Yankees. This is how the Red Sox fan sees himself.

In the late autumn of 2003, true believers of Red Sox Nation needed to glean meaning from everything. Rain—and it always seemed to rain—was an omen. Somebody had to explain exactly how events had gotten this far. The gray skies clouded the recent canvas of leafy greens and rich yellows, smothering the brightness and possibility of the summer. As the miserable ending of the 2003 baseball season coincided with skeletal trees and an encompassing silence in a town where only days before there had been so much noise, the true believers felt not overdramatic but in sync with Nature. In their eyes, the weather was, after all, mourning with Boston.

That is the kind of poetic despair that overtakes Boston when its heroes fail, and why in a country that is becoming curiously, and in many parts bitterly, ambivalent toward the billion-dollar sports industry, Boston is still awash with passion, willfully giving itself over to the hyperbole, the drama.

Over the spring and summer and fall of 2003, the Red Sox had cajoled, teased, tantalized, and romanced their city, and finally when they had convinced the city to believe, to ascend high, the team fell hard. And the city with it. The Boston Red Sox came fingernail-close to reaching the World Series, to beating the New York Yankees, who, along with history, are their greatest tormentors. But the Red Sox didn't win. They lost, and while someone always must, the reaction, overheated and self-indulgent as it was, still represented the best and worst of Boston as a sports city.

The intensity and overreaction makes fans in other cities alternately envy and loathe Boston, and shake their heads at the city's heady and inflated sense of self. Boston fans are a community of true believers, for whom a flower dying in the cold is less a natural occurrence than proof that the higher authorities also considered the end of the season a devastating event. Oh come on, was it that bad? For them, it was, but to understand how a collection of sports fans crumple at defeat and often have difficulty enjoying victory is to connect with the inner mind of the New Englander. It seems to me that Boston worries, as some people also do, about giving more than it receives, of being smart but maybe not smart enough, of needing that favorable comparison, needing to be superior, which explains to some degree why losses seem to hurt more here. Such personal tics create myopia, and many fans overlook the simple truth: that the cycle of winning and losing is no different here in Boston than anywhere else.

The local sports compact is an all-or-nothing emotional attachment, and with rare exception this deal is binding—which is pleasing to men in suits with deep pockets, the owners whose wallets thrive on this emotional grist of the sports industry. The fan who signs his name on such a document is a person like my old friend Mike

Comeau, who was able, finally, to confront the contract during a wonderful, searching, and euphoric stream-of-consciousness digression that followed Boston's first Super Bowl win, when the formerly ignominious New England Patriots won the trophy in February 2002. "I don't understand it," Mike said, "I've given everything I have to this team, and I guess I should know better, but I don't. But then I think about people who don't get excited for sports, who don't care that much if a team wins or loses, and during times like right now, I think of how much they miss! Why does this matter so much? Why do we make these, these...investments? Why do we care so much about this?" That's Boston.

But so is this: The Boston fan will dress from top to toe in the team colors, skip work, spend a fortune on the big game, and yet, in the smoldering heat of the fight, when hardiness is a must, deflate at the first sign of trouble: "I knew they were going to lose." What creates this jarring combination of chauvinism and defeatism in Boston? It is a question the hip-hop virtuoso Eminem answered while discussing a wholly unrelated subject: "You got to live it to feel it, [if] you didn't then you wouldn't get it."

This collision of confidence and despair is what the Red Sox fan is, despite himself. He doesn't want to be the sad-sack doomsayer who always "knows" the Sox are going to lose, even in the fourth inning of a scoreless game, but he can't handle the weight and unpredictability of faith. She doesn't want to be that perverse double agent who takes joy in the continuing heartbreak, yet tells all her friends that the Sox will "blow it again" at the end. He doesn't want to be the know-it-all who plays "second-guess the manager" after every tough Red Sox loss, one who constructs heroes, glorifies their achievements, makes them one of us, only to tear them down, brick by brick, when they ultimately fail. He doesn't want to be associated with the uncomfortable social dynamic, part of the subtle barricade that separates black and white, a divide that defines the city as surely as the Longfellow Bridge. We all want to be above those individual and not always flattering ingredients that nourish sports in Boston, to somehow claim the passion and not the shadows. In short, some of us want to be a clean fuel, the energy that can drive a locomotive without creating air pollution. Whether this is possible? Who knows.

Boston's truly special claim is not, in my view, as the home of long-suffering fans, nor fans more knowledgeable and passionate than, say, those in Pittsburgh. Boston rises in importance for being perhaps the only city in America in which sports teams still serve as a mirror of the best and worst of the city—reflecting both admirable elements that Bostonians rightly celebrate, and traits that we lament and would prefer to ignore.

Boston is famous, equally, for abolition and racism, for social justice and busing riots, for vision and inflexibility—interconnected strains that can be felt while walking around town, or in the box seats at Fenway Park, where the Red Sox live, or at the Fleet Center, home of the basketball Celtics and hockey Bruins. The city is famous for its oft-stated desire to confront these stubborn contradictions, and for its only limited success in doing so.

In a sense, Boston's ideals and history make it paradigmatic of the human, especially American, challenge of forever aspiring to be better than we are—and the temptation to elevate Boston into something more than just another sports town. It is this challenge, to live up to its special pedigree and grow from its racial contradictions and failures, to harness its expectations, that separates Boston from the Philadelphias, Seattles, and Dallases of the sports world and transform passion into constructive energy.

The elevation of the Celtics came about not only because of big names like the Cooz (Bob Cousy), Bill Russell, Tommy Heinsohn, and John Havlicek, or the bushel of championship trophies. For both blacks and whites in Boston, the Celtics also represented a mythology of hope without politics, a team on which the recognition of merit was not a lofty ideal, but a practice. This depth, this elevation of ideal, is the difference between the Celtic experience and that of the Minneapolis Lakers, basketball's first dynasty. The Lakers were just a basketball team; when a better one came along, their significance waned.

During the 1960s, the time of the Celtics, blacks demanded, if nothing else, an opportunity, and in response, the Celtics began to break the old, unspoken rules of American basketball. In Boston, in 1967, Bill Russell became the first black coach in the history of integrated American team sports. The Celtics had already shattered the old custom of maintaining a white majority on the playing floor by fielding an entirely black starting lineup. A decade earlier, the Celtics had signed Chuck Cooper, the first black player drafted in the league. Red Auerbach, a Celtics patriarch, profited from that spirit of change. He saw life in the honorific terms of merit, crusty and simple. If you could play, you would be given a chance. That's it. That was the hope.

And the Celtics would win, which was the ultimate proof of Auerbach's smart decisions. That was the Boston of ideals, the Boston that long before the Civil War had opened its hospitals to blacks, a policy then heresy in the rest of a nation encumbered by racial injustice. That was the Boston that articulated a civic credo of brotherhood, of integrated schools and public transportation, universities and theater, the city that slaves heard about, dreamed about, and around which they planned their escapes.

This Boston remains today, unbowed, a place where a neighborly, democratic ethos still watches and broods in the face of harsh, painful realities. Walk along the Fens, around its curves and the jut of Boylston Street toward the Prudential Center and you will come upon the stern, mustachioed bust of John Boyle O'Reilly, the Irish poet-activist who more than a century ago sought unity between Boston's blacks and its emerging Irish population. Along Columbus Avenue, in the city's South End, there is a bronze marker for the Underground Railroad, and at the top of Boston Common, directly across from the State House, a bronze bas-relief honors the Fifty-fourth Regiment, the Civil War's most recognizable symbol of black bravery.

These emblems of Boston's hopes for social and racial justice are legitimate. But the more complicated story, the whole story, requires a hardiness of a different sort, the ability to look at an unpleasant reflection in the mirror. Despite the championships, white Bostonians never fully embraced the black superstars of the Celtics, Bill Russell, especially. There is a reason for that. Auerbach, more shrewd than noble, understood the undercurrent of the city, and was keenly aware of another, less desirable truth: that white fans—the true economic engine of any sports franchise—did not entirely cotton to basketball as a game as much as they identified with white basketball players. Thus, by design, the Celtics dynasty of the 1980s was constructed as the most racially balanced team in the NBA, consistently, a fact that did not elude the eyes of the members of a league that, by 1985, was nearly 80 percent black. Fielding ten white players on a roster in the NBA, as the Celtics did in the championship year of 1986, it should be noted, is a very difficult thing to do. Thus, if the idealistic Celtics of the 1960s would speak for Boston, so too does the monument of the 1980s teams.

Boston was never quite the haven that school textbooks claimed, and both O'Reilly and former Kentucky slave Lewis Hayden—who escaped to Boston and turned his house into an important Underground Railroad station—failed in those faraway days of trying to build bridges between Boston's Irish and black citizens. The lack of bridges was revealed starkly in subsequent generations, in the explosive 1970s of school desegregation, and also long before, in simmering feuds during more muted decades. Yankee Boston retrenched, controlling the money, while Irish and black Boston circled one another, both groups fighting with mounting resentments for the same bite-size morsel, the same lousy jobs, the same limited place. Their common enemy was, and is, a system of power, one so formidable and stealthy that instead of fighting it, they fought each other.

That sports could intersect at all with a city's legacy gave it special appeal, for the same arguments cannot be made, for example, with the Miami Dolphins, or even with the Yankees. As much as these intersections of race and class in sports heighten the Boston narrative, they also help us to scrutinize it. The power forward for the Phoenix Suns is not often asked, for example, for his perspectives on race relations, as his counterpart in Boston surely is. Race and notions of race permeate the game, more so in Boston because of the unresolved questions, and also perhaps due to the admirable, but largely unsuccessful quest by citizens like O'Reilly, Garrison, and Douglass to build lasting dialogue between white and blacks in Boston. Today, the collective local tendency—by weary, stubborn fans; a timid, frustrated media; and the revenue-conscious teams—is simply to pretend no such subtext exists. When the burgeoning new rivals, the New Jersey Nets, and the Celtics play, a delicate racial tension exists in the stands and in the minds of the New Jersey players, who view Boston warily. It is felt with each foul, three-pointer, and lead change.

The player of color who comes to Boston recognizes this no-win dynamic immediately and must chart a strategy of dealing with the fan who will accept him only by following the prepared script, without much improvisation. In that script, the person of color must run hard to first base or risk the wrath of a region uninterested in analyzing its own double standard. He must keep his mouth shut. He also knows why such a standard exists, that the old bitterness will resurface until there is dialogue (and results). The Boston Red Sox were the last team to integrate the major leagues, in 1959. Had they not humiliated Jackie Robinson in a 1945 tryout, they could have been the first. Under the famously racist Tom Yawkey (who has a street named after him, as well as a lounge at Boston's Logan International Airport, and a venerable charitable trust), the Red Sox organization did not employ a single black person from 1956 until 1959—not a janitor, not a secretary, not a groundskeeper, and certainly not a player. In the mid-1970s, when every player in baseball was available for a price, the Red Sox (now under Yawkey's widow, Jean) chose to sign no black players on the open free-agent market; nor did they in the 1980s. Black baseball players, knowing their power, and what they might be getting into, have often refused to be traded to Boston.

Do the fans who call themselves part of Red Sox Nation truly want to be claimed by the object of their passion, or just by portions of it? This is the contradiction, the problem with mirrors. If we truly want to fuel the locomotive, to be the fans who make Boston the sports city it is, then we must claim the weighty grievances that also define Boston. The two cannot be separated. This is the price of being a true Red Sox fan. In Boston, history is a heavy document to carry. Should you redefine "Red Sox fan" to include being aware of the history and committed to healing Boston's racial issues via sports, as much as that is possible?

\*   \*   \*

Not long after October 17 rolled around, the first day of baseball's winter, and the day wind sliced around the city, making it hell for everyone who had neglected to wear a heavier coat, Pedro

Martinez, the ace pitcher of the Red Sox, was at home in Santo Domingo, his Dominican Republic hometown, trying to articulate the uncomfortable feeling that was gnawing at him. Over the course of the season, he threw 2,838 pitches, 498 more during an epic playoff run. A total of 2,724,165 people had come to Fenway Park—a 100.2 percent capacity, a staggering statement of popularity, even before the exhilarating series between the Sox and Oakland A's, the games that were the undercard to the Red Sox–Yankees main event. Both the Oakland/Sox and Sox/Yankee series exceeded prior billing, and for once the highbrowed literary set of baseball fans wasn't blowing smoke with the suggestion that there was treasure to be found at the ballpark.

In the aftermath—after an offensively challenged pinch-hitter named Aaron Boone hit the game-winning home run in the eleventh inning of game seven of the American League Championship Series, ending the Red Sox's season and putting the Yankees in the World Series—the house seemed to win again. The all-or-nothing compact that New England signs with its baseball club had turned up snake eyes, and there were no words that could adequately capture the moment of losing.

During a rare easy moment in the Red Sox–Yankees series, the question arose in the dugout, among the pregame chatter, of whether even in defeat to the Yankees the season could be considered a success. The answer, at first, seemed to be an immediate yes, for over the 2003 season, Red Sox baseball had done something that is immensely hard for any team to do over the full course of a season: The Red Sox captured the collective imagination. The legions of fans that poured into the ballpark didn't go just out of habit. They were actually taken with this team, with its relentless style of play, and Boston fans were very open to being seduced. In 2003 they embraced a season-defining slogan and song—"Cowboy Up!"; there was a heightened energy at the ballpark, and then the rising belief, stoked by a willing media, that there actually could be a cherry on the top of this sundae, that there was good reason to believe that this was the year. Baseball was fun, and even the impulse to expect defeat had waned.

Yet when Mr. Boone's ball landed in the left-field seats, the customary reflection and softening that is an important part of losing did not occur in Red Sox Nation. Curiously, fans did not take the consolations of fond remembrance; the pleasure of recollecting the wonders of the season and the players might have sprouted, armistice-like, in the next day, or the next week, or the next month, but it did not. The youthful energy that had swept Boston all summer had simply been extinguished, and instead of grateful memories of a season that delivered our city enjoyment and fun to burn, there seemed to be anger—at the particular players in the drama, at the manager Grady Little, and of course at the Yankees, for being better, again. I could see that some fans were wondering whether the whole roller-coaster journey had been worth it. Wasn't the thrilling season of David Ortiz, Kevin Millar, Bill Mueller, and Jason Varitek the epitome of what my friend Mike Comeau meant by investment? Here is the question, and not only for Boston fans: As people who love sports, is our emotional investment in the journey of the season meaningful only if our team produces the ultimate return, the big win? For the idea of sport to remain powerful in the imagination, the journey must always be worth it.

Yet a whole tremendous season seemed voided by losing. The reasons to be wistful—that amazing ninth-inning comeback in April, the horrible loss followed by another heart-stopping win that restored our faith, and again, that delicious Friday afternoon in July when the Sox pounded the Yankees—instead became sources of anger, or dismissal. The city and team packed up its house of summer very swiftly; the manager was sacked, and his name, in a sense, erased from the credits of an exuberant year. Some players were dumped; others, to rid the team of expensive contracts, were offered away for free. Even the best players, like Nomar Garciaparra and the great Martinez, players who own the institutional memory that connects team to fan, father to son, at least in theory, were made to feel expendable because of their pending free agency and the hunt for sexy new faces, among them the great shortstop Alex Rodriguez and pitcher Curt Schilling. The focus on the loss seemed to render the season meaningless and its players interchangeable. How different the city would have felt in October if fans could savor what a win it is for any team to be one of the four best teams in baseball.

A couple of weeks later, baseball revealed that 5 to 7 percent of players tested positive for the use of anabolic steroids, which meant that dozens of players had used drugs in the hope of making themselves hit better, run and throw faster, be stronger and more attractive to teams—that dozens of players were cheating. Slightly aroused, the public did not seem properly outraged that its heroes were cheating. John Henry, the principal owner of the Red Sox, and Pedro Martinez and other Red Sox thinkers, expressed the view that the journey of sports, the summer-long chapters that unfold and give the game importance, had been diminished not by losing the series, but by the winning-at-all-costs mentality indicated by the widespread drug use. Perhaps the anger that the 2003 Red Sox did not win is almost inevitable in a society in which the bottom lines of profit and scores so often trump other rewards, like loyalty and integrity.

With a diminished value on the journey itself, and our investment in the pleasures of that journey, Boston is in danger of being less of a sports city—even as its passions rise—for without the investment, the experience of sports becomes thin, attenuated to only one standard, one challenge—providing victory, not necessarily pleasure. The journey, and its long-term implication, perhaps, lost its fire from the belief that the fan cares more than the player ever did (always the case), that the diehard has finally recognized his mistake in caring about the details and the players who simply change teams, allegiances, and tax brackets every year. Certainly, this possibility seemed true with the Red Sox, who brought the fan close, and are poised to look completely different next year, and especially the year after. Even in 1986, when the ball went through Buckner's legs, Red Sox fans knew they had the long career of Roger Clemens to look forward to, and slowly came to the conclusion that the team did its best.

This withering of consistency from year to year intrinsically devalues the journey against the results, for the names always change. Chris Wallace, an executive with the Celtics, identified this phenomenon, too, saying, "People no longer see a player's name on the back of his jersey. They only see the number of zeroes on his contract. [The players] are dangerously close to not being people anymore." Perhaps this explains why there was little acknowledgment that the Red Sox made summer fun—which is their task—and why nobody seemed to care that the drug kit instead of the gym was creating a group of superathletes. It didn't matter how the home runs were hit, as long as they were. The journey of winning, once the foundation of victory, seemed secondary to victory itself, no matter how it was achieved.

The result of such pressure systems is an inevitable collision between the cynical forces that have come to chip at the meaningfulness of sports and that lusty commitment of the Boston diehard sports fan, fortified by generations, happily seduced into the silky illusion that sports carry daily value. It is the welcome acceptance of this illusion, that the fan is in fact a living part of the illusion every day, for life, and not the ephemeral nature of the final score, that makes us look forward to next year. In other words, you've got to live it to feel it.

# Bridging Difference:
# We're All Here Now

*Anita Diamant*

I came to Boston in 1975 to be a poet. I was twenty-four and Boston seemed a likely place to wear that invisible hat—a city with a great literary history and dozens of bookstores. It was also a beautiful city, with brownstones and brick sidewalks and, whenever I turned around, a flash of harbor or river winking back at the four-season sky.

Of course, there is no living to be made in poetry, so I became a journalist, freelancing my way into the alternative press and then to mainstream newspapers and magazines. I learned my trade on the job, which also provided me a passkey to the city. I had access to hospital rooms, prison cells, gymnasiums, restaurant kitchens, theater wings, convent halls. I met movers, shakers, thinkers, and some of the secret saints that keep the heart of the world from breaking in two. Along the way, I fell in love for keeps with a man who was not Jewish.

When I moved to Boston, I was Jewish the way that I am blue eyed; a defining feature, innate but mostly unselfconscious. But with marriage in sight, I realized that I very much wanted our eventual offspring to claim my birthright. I didn't fully understand why it mattered so much to me, though, nor had I any idea about how to pass it along.

So I engineered some assignments for articles about the Jewish community and visited its synagogues, classrooms, boardrooms, and shops. I interviewed scholars, rabbis, community leaders, artists, and found myself amid a thirsty crowd of adult learners, all trying to figure out why Judaism mattered to them too. I had found my spiritual home.

In Boston, of all places. Home of the Yankee bean and cod, where the crucifix casts a very long shadow. Well, maybe it isn't so odd. The city was founded by people who refused to settle for anything less than a life that was a complete and authentic expression of their faith. They wagered their fortunes and their families for that dream, in an unforgiving climate. Why couldn't a wandering/wondering Jew get comfortable amid that history?

Sure, Boston has been infamous for parochialism and intolerance historically: plays banned, the Irish treated like dogs, schoolchildren stoned for the color of their skin. But this is, at root, an Old Testament city where the soul is the perennial subject of honored debate, and where injustice is ultimately recognized as sin.

The South is widely considered the religious epicenter of the United States, and yet the search for God at Harvard predates the buckling of the Bible Belt and it has never stopped. The Boston area gave rise to Congregationalism, transcendentalism, and Christian Science. An abundance of venerable seminaries and divinity schools coexist along the Charles, and nearly all of them are on speaking terms.

And we're all here now: Muslims and Buddhists, Eastern Orthodox, Baptists, Evangelicals, cheek by jowl with the Catholics and Unitarians. In immigrant neighborhoods, hymns are sung in Creole, Portuguese, Vietnamese, all obeying the Psalmist's invitation to "Sing unto God a new song."

You can't walk through the city upon a hill without noticing that there are many different paths up the holy mountain. Maybe it's easier where everyone is using the same prayer book, but this rich religious stew is a great attraction to the spiritually secure. And I think it's good for the Jews.

* * *

The metropolitan Boston area is home to the sixth largest Jewish community in the United States. Still, Jewish life here retains a small-town feel, probably because everyone is connected by only two or three degrees of separation. The lines tend to cross denominational boundaries and many run through the city's universities. Over the years, charismatic rabbis—from Soloveitchik and Twersky to the Kushners (Harold and Lawrence, no relation)—have attracted acolytes who stayed, studied, published, and taught.

In the self-proclaimed Athens of America, Jewish learning is a growth industry. Preschools and day schools abound. Lectures, panel discussions, concerts, and readings crowd the calendar. Lawyers and social workers, new mommies and retirees enroll in Torah study classes all over the city, from early morning to late in the evening, seven days a week.

I would argue that Boston is the contemporary incarnation of Yavneh, which became the center of the Jewish universe after the destruction of Jerusalem nearly two thousand years ago. This is a comparison dripping with chutzpah, if not hubris, but I am not the only one in town willing to make this audacious case: In the year 70, the Romans razed the holy Temple in Jerusalem, scattered the population, and forever ended the traditions of pilgrimages, priests, and fiery rites. The conquered Israelites and their invisible God seemed doomed to extinction. But the sages and leaders of Jerusalem fled to a small town called Yavneh, home of Rabbi Yochanan ben Zakkai, who reconstituted Jerusalem's Sanhedrin—a "supreme court" of seventy-one sages and judges—in his vineyard. There, they created a new Jewish praxis based on prayer, study, and ethics. The final canon of the Hebrew Bible was settled upon in Yavneh, and what we know as Judaism was born.

Until the twentieth century, the destruction of the Temple was the defining tragedy of the Jewish people, the touchstone of loss and longing. But after the Nazis murdered so many Jews, burned so many books, sacked so many synagogues, and looted so many souls, the earlier conflagration was eclipsed by that unspeakable darkness.

Out of those ashes, the state of Israel represented a tangible hope for security and continuity. There is a vibrant intellectual and cultural life in Israel, but there is also blood in the streets of Jerusalem, and funerals, and too much fear to permit the fullest flowering of Jewish life. May that day come soon.

\* \* \*

You might think New York City would be the most likely place for a modern Yavneh. It is home to more Jews than anywhere else on the planet, but it's just too big, diffuse, and self-satisfied to spearhead something as tender as a spiritual revival. Besides, New York doesn't have to "do" anything to "be" Jewish. Lenny Bruce, the philosopher-fool, once famously divided the world in two: Jewish and goyish. "Fruit salad is Jewish," Bruce explained. "Lime Jell-O is goyish."

"If you live in New York, you are Jewish," he said. "It doesn't matter even if you're Catholic; if you live in New York, you're Jewish. If you live in Butte, Montana, you're going to be goyish, even if you're Jewish."

You've got to work at being Jewish in goyish Boston. Solomon Franco, the first Jew to land in Massachusetts Bay in 1649, was "warned out" of town, and it took another two hundred years before things warmed up for his kinsmen. The coincidence of a labor shortage and a wave of German Jewish immigration in the mid-1800s gave the community its real start, and by the 1920s there were seven Yiddish newspapers in town and hundreds of self-help and charity organizations, from banks to burial societies to baseball teams.

Anti-Semitism has simmered and flared in Boston over the years. Beth Israel Hospital was founded in 1916, spearheaded by an army of Jewish women who refused to brook the internship quotas that kept their sons from medical training. The broadcasts of Father Charles E. Coughlin in the 1930s and Father Leonard Feeney in the 1950s encouraged physical attacks on Jews in the neighborhoods. And "white-shoe" downtown law firms quietly practiced exclusionary employment practices right up to the 1960s.

Even so, Jewish neighborhoods flourished, first in the South End, then in the North End, the West End, and out into Roxbury, Dorchester, and Mattapan. Today there are communities in Brookline, Sharon, and nearly every suburb. Along the way, Boston Jews became Bostonians, assimilating into the surrounding culture and ultimately becoming leaders and supporters of institutions and organizations from which their parents had been banned. In a city that prides itself on its firsts (first public school, post office, public library, subway, streetlight, use of penicillin, department store), Boston's Jews have a similar list: the first unified charity, which became the model for the United Way; the first bureau of Jewish education, the first schools of modern Hebrew; the first Hebrew teachers college.

That tradition didn't end in the nineteenth century either; witness Facing History and Ourselves, the Holocaust-education program; the Jewish Women's Coalition on Breast Cancer; and the Gay, Lesbian, Bisexual, and Transgendered Group of Combined Jewish Philanthropies, that oldest of national "umbrella" charities. Boston fostered the Jewish Women's Archive, the first on-line "library" devoted to telling that mostly untold story, and Me'ah, a citywide adult Jewish literacy project, and Mayyim Hayyim Living Waters Community Mikveh and Education Center, which reinvents the ancient mystery of ritual immersion for Jews, many of whose great-grandparents abandoned the institution and practice when they crossed the Atlantic.This is a woefully incomplete list, which will land me in hot water for not mentioning a dozen other growing-edge projects while including the mikveh that (full disclosure) I helped to found. It is an amazing chapter of Jewish history, this glittering Yankee-Yavneh moment. I count myself blessed to be part of it.

Not that it's all milk and honey in Beantown. The Jews have gone native in some less-than-attractive ways. Newcomers may find us relatively reserved, if not downright cool. And, like the rest of Massachusetts' citizenry, we are at the bottom of national rankings when it comes to charitable giving. We still lack for indigenous rye bread, pickles, or pastrami worthy of the heartburn. There is far more sectarian squabbling than anyone cares to admit.

But all of that pales when you look up at the bridge.

Its full name is the Leonard P. Zakim Bunker Hill Bridge. The gorgeous 180-foot span pays tribute to the revolutionary war memorial in Charlestown, but its first name honors the memory of the regional director of the Anti-Defamation League who died in 1999, after a long battle against cancer. In his twenty years at ADL, Lenny (no one called him anything else) was famous for his passionate commitment to equality, his sense of humor, and his genius for making friends and creating coalitions with people of every color, creed, and political persuasion. Zakim's death was mourned by the whole city. But this soaring sculpture of a bridge—echoing the Charlestown obelisk, summoning images of open books and furled sails—is not a cenotaph. It is a pledge to continue Lenny's work of building bridges. It is a promise to live up to Lenny's dream, which is both the promise of America and the covenant of the Jews: justice. Justice for all.

## ACKNOWLEDGMENTS

Every book has a story behind it, and this one most certainly does. It begins with an idea that first came out of a conversation I had with former Bank Boston chief economist Jim Howell, who now does economic consulting in the city. Both Jim and I have ties to Texas, although his are deep and abiding while mine were of the kind that journalists develop when they land in a new city on a new assignment—several miles wide and, by their nature, not very deep. When Jim learned of my short stint as managing editor of the *Fort Worth Star-Telegram* in the late 1980s, he started grilling me about which Texas writers I knew and had worked with. Soon we had expanded our scope to include the rest of the South (although *true* Texans generally don't see themselves as part of any regional constellation except their own). Because our conversation occurred the day after Boston had landed the bid to become the site of the 2004 Democratic National Convention and because we had already determined that we had a mutual friend in Bill Kovach, Jim mentioned that when Bill was editor of the *Atlanta Journal-Constitution*, he used the occasion of the 1988 Democratic convention in that city to publish in the newspaper a collection of essays about the South by well-known southern writers. He thought the delegates attending the convention needed a literary primer on what made the South the unique and beguiling region that it is.

What a wonderful idea, I thought, tucking it away. As someone who has been a senior editor at major metropolitan dailies throughout the United States, Bill's project celebrated my two passions—the urban landscape and a love of good writing. Few would argue with the claim that if the South has a rival for the most literary region in this country, it would have to be New England—specifically Boston. The city has inspired and launched some of the brightest literary lights in history, and still provides a nourishing environment for writers.

Sadly, Boston does not have a strong reputation for nurturing *all* of its residents. Even though tremendous progress has been made since the painful school-desegregation days of the 1970s, the city is still thought of by many people as a racially divided one. It also has a reputation for being a little stuffy and old fashioned, even parochial.

Moving here in 1997 to serve as editor and vice chairman of Community Newspaper Company, I was delighted to find a *new* Boston— one of the most diverse, innovative, and beautiful cities in the world. It has its problems, but it tackles them through a surprisingly resilient series of multisector partnerships. The city has one of the liveliest arts and cultural sectors of any in the country—and, of course, brilliant writers, some of whom generously agreed to participate in this anthology.

In my current role at the Boston Foundation, I found myself in the perfect position to act on the idea I had tucked away for just the right moment—and suggest that the Boston Foundation sponsor an anthology of Boston authors presenting a fresh portrait of this wonderful city, to be published on the occasion of the 2004 Democratic National Convention in Boston. The foundation's president, Paul Grogan—a longtime observer and passionate advocate for the importance of cities—saw the project as a powerful gift the foundation could make to Boston at a time when the city would take its place at the center of the world's stage. When I mentioned the idea to Barbara Hindley, longtime senior editor of the Boston Foundation, she said she knew the perfect editor to make it happen. Emily Hiestand, a widely admired and award-winning essayist herself, was the ideal person to take the idea and shape it into the book you hold in your hands. Inspired by the concept, Emily accepted the role, and asked a colleague, Ande Zellman, the highly regarded publishing executive and former editor of the *Boston Sunday Globe Magazine*, to serve with her as coeditor.

As our book team contemplated the full spectrum of voices, perspectives, and themes that could be at home in this volume, we realized that our list, in its entirety, could easily generate a whole series of books. Although from the beginning we envisioned this anthology as a collage of the city, a portrait in time, and certainly not a definitive tome, winnowing our roster to only fifteen authors proved to be a formidable challenge. After much reflection and consultation, Emily and Ande began to invite both noted and emerging voices within the Boston literary community—including essayists, literary journalists, and fiction writers—to participate in a project that called on them as citizens as well as talented artists. Emily and Barbara Hindley, who played a key role at every stage of this project, introduced the foundation to Jill Kneerim of the Kneerim and Williams Literary Agency. Jill loved the book concept at once and approached Helene Atwan, director of Beacon Press, to be the publisher. Helene's strong support was invaluable in moving the book forward, and Beacon's commitment included bringing executive editor Joanne Wyckoff into the project to offer her expert guidance. Beacon Press and the Boston Foundation share many of the same values, including a deep commitment to diversity, social justice, and the power of imagination to bring about change. The collaboration that emerged between Beacon Press and the Boston Foundation as we created this book together is an additional boon of the project.

It is a testament to Emily, Ande, Barbara, Jill, Helene, and Joanne —as well as a tribute to the reputations of the Boston Foundation and Beacon Press—that the stellar writers included in this anthology agreed, enthusiastically, to participate in a book project that offered them a breathtakingly tight deadline and modest financial remuneration. Their dedication to this book most certainly reflects their own deep love for Boston and their willingness to engage in the ongoing work of building "the good city."

I don't think that the *truly* good city ever is a static one; rather, it is one that is constantly engaged in a never-ending process of be-coming a far better city. This anthology is the result of the energy and goodwill of many talented people who felt inspired on behalf of a city they care about deeply, and it is also, perhaps, a testament to the power of an idea—brought forward at just the right time.

**Mary Jo Meisner**
*Vice President for Communications,*
*Community Relations, and Public Affairs*
*The Boston Foundation*

# CONTRIBUTORS

**Jack Beatty** is a senior editor at the *Atlantic Monthly* and a news analyst for National Public Radio's *On Point*. He is author of *Colossus: How the Corporation Changed America* and *The Rascal King: The Life and Times of James Michael Curley (1874–1958)*. He lives in Hanover, New Hampshire.

**Howard Bryant** is a senior sportswriter for the *Boston Herald* and author of *Shut Out: The Story of Race and Baseball in Boston*. He lives in Boston.

**Robert Campbell** is a Pulitzer Prize–winning writer and architect. He is architecture critic for the *Boston Globe* and a contributing editor and columnist for *Architectural Record*. He is author of *Cityscapes of Boston: An American City through Time*. He lives and works in Cambridge, Massachusetts.

**Alan Chong** is curator of the collection at the Isabella Stewart Gardner Museum. He is editor of a volume of essays titled *Rethinking Rembrandt* and coeditor of *Eye of the Beholder: Masterpieces from the Isabella Stewart Gardner Museum*.

**Anita Diamant** is author of *The Red Tent* and *Good Harbor*. She is also the author of six nonfiction guides to Jewish life and a collection of essays titled *Pitching My Tent: On Marriage, Motherhood, Friendship, and Other Leaps of Faith.* She lives in Newton, Massachusetts.

**Paul S. Grogan** is coauthor of *Comeback Cities: A Blueprint for Urban Neighborhood Revival* and president and CEO of the Boston Foundation.

**Derrick Z. Jackson,** a columnist for the *Boston Globe,* was a Pulitzer finalist in 2001, a two-time winner from the National Education Writers Association, and a five-time winner from the National Association of Black Journalists.

**Jane Holtz Kay** is the architecture critic for the *Nation.* She is the author of *Asphalt Nation: How the Automobile Took Over America and How We Can Take It Back; Preserving New England;* and *Lost Boston.* She lives in Boston.

**Scott Kirsner** is a contributing editor at *Fast Company Magazine* and writes a weekly column for the *Boston Globe.* He lives in Cambridge, Massachusetts.

**Michael Patrick MacDonald** is author of *All Souls: A Family Story from Southie,* which won an American Book Award. He is a recipient of the 1999 Daily Points of Light Award and the New England Literary Lights Award. He currently lives in Brooklyn, New York.

**James Miller** is editor of *Daedalus,* the journal of the American Academy of Arts and Sciences, in Cambridge, Massachusetts, and also professor of political science at the New School for Social Research, in New York City. His books include *Flowers in the Dustbin: The Rise of Rock & Roll, 1947–1977; The Passion of Michel Foucault;* and *"Democracy Is in the Streets": From Port Huron to the Siege of Chicago.* He lives in New York City.

**John Hanson Mitchell** is the author of numerous books, including *Ceremonial Time: Fifteen Thousand Years of One Square Mile* and *Following the Sun: A Bicycle Pilgrimage from Andalusia to the Hebrides.* He is also editor of *Sanctuary,* a magazine published by the Massachusetts Audubon Society. He lives in Littleton, Massachusetts.

**Lynda Morgenroth** has written on art, architecture, and urban culture; nature and the environment; and social issues. She is author of *Boston*

*Neighborhoods: A Food Lover's Walking, Eating, and Shopping Guide to Ethnic Enclaves in and around Boston* and is a contributing author of *Toward the Livable City*. She lives in Melrose, Massachusetts.

**Susan Orlean** has been a staff writer at the *New Yorker* since 1992 and has contributed to many other magazines. She is author of *The Orchid Thief,* which was made into the film *Adaptation,* and numerous volumes of collected essays. Currently, she is a fellow at the Nieman Foundation of Harvard University. She lives in Boston.

**Patricia Powell** is the author of *Me Dying Trial, A Small Gathering of Bones, The Pagoda,* and a forthcoming novel, *The Good Life.* She is the Martin Luther King Visiting Professor of Creative Writing at Massachusetts Institute of Technology. She lives in Watertown, Massachusetts.

**Irene Smalls** is a storyteller and the author of numerous children's books, including *Kevin and His Dad; Jonathan and His Mommy;* and *Irene and the Big, Fine Nickel.* She lives in Boston with her three children, Dawn, Kevin Logan, and Jonathan.